SAINTS IN APRONS

SAINTS
in APRONS

by ROSE M. HUESMAN

THE BRUCE PUBLISHING COMPANY • MILWAUKEE

NIHIL OBSTAT: 76497

    JOHN F. MURPHY, S.T.D.
    Censor librorum

IMPRIMATUR:

    ✠WILLIAM E. COUSINS
    Archbishop of Milwaukee

    October 27, 1961

Library of Congress Catalog Card Number: 62–10343

© 1962 THE BRUCE PUBLISHING COMPANY
MADE IN THE UNITED STATES OF AMERICA

To Our Lady of Good Counsel
AND TO ALL MOTHERS EVERYWHERE
WHO WANT TO FOLLOW
IN HER FOOTSTEPS

ACKNOWLEDGMENT

All scriptural passages used are from the Douay version of the Bible. Liturgical excerpts are from the Roman Missal.

With sincere gratitude, the author wishes to acknowledge the help and encouragement of all those interested in seeing this work published; especially the charitable and patient Passionist Fathers of St. Joseph's Passionist Monastery in Baltimore, Maryland.

PREFACE

Marriage is sacred. It is not man's idea at all. It is God's. Not on earth are we to find its origin but in heaven. Handled only as an earthy thing marriage falls apart. When marriage falls apart families are broken; homes are disrupted. The young hearts of children are seared for life. The Church is wounded. Nations subverted. This is catastrophe.

Left to themselves a man and a woman cannot manage marriage. The heroicity, the constancy, the courage, the endless love — these are more than weak human nature can bring forth. The recurrent breakdown in family living is sad witness to this truth. And how many couples there are whose marriage is anything but sacred and lovable. Even though they avoid the ultimate collapse, their marriage is nothing more than an agreed truce; the pursuit of their individual lives while they are residing at the same address. In one case a couple with three children decided to "keep the marriage together" but neither would consent to be in the house as long as the other was there.

The attempt to make marriage click apart from God and faith is bound to end in failure. Taking marriage as a purely human thing will eventually dehumanize it. For marriage is divine or it is inexplicable. It is too sublime to entrust to human keeping. God must have a hand in marriage. Indeed, He must become the very heart and center of marriage. Who better understands man and woman than He who made them? Who formed the body of man? Who gave beauty to woman? Who gave to both an immortal soul with all its dignity? Who entrusted life to their keeping? Who then can be more necessary to them?

It was no insignificant action on Christ's part to make of marriage matrimony. Human love was changed forever when Christ placed it in the company of the most sacred realities known to man — the sacraments. Just as a young man kneeling before the altar on his ordination day arises as someone different, changed, ennobled, consecrated, so in a similar way a young lover and his bride kneeling before Christ on their wedding day become something more than just man and wife. They are changed. They are ennobled. They are consecrated, made sacred. And again as the new priest takes bread and wine into his sacred hands and through the power of his ordination changes them into the Body and Blood of Christ, so in a similar way husband and wife take the daily, ordinary, routine actions that make up married life and, through the power of their sacrament, elevate them, give them a new meaning — supernatural acts worthy of eternal merit. This is so because matrimony relates husband and wife to God in a special way. Coming back to us from the altar, hand in hand, God presents them to the world as consecrated lovers, founders of a family, sanctifiers of life. They have His blessing upon their joint lives. His divine power is in them to sanctify every step of that journey down the aisle, out into the world, and through all of life's pathways until their last breath and that final step into eternity.

This is marriage as God remade it; marriage that is fruitful in children whose clear eyes and pure hearts and integral lives reflect not only the physical qualities but also, and especially, the spiritual attainments of their parents. Marriage fruitful in grace begets that equilibrium and harmony, that peace and love which characterize the Christian home. This is magnificence.

Is this an unattainable ideal? Is it too much for you? This book shows that it is not too much for you and that it is not an unattainable ideal. The ideal can be attained but not through marriage alone. It must be marriage in Christ.

The wedding ring placed on your finger is the sign of your love. But when, during the marriage ceremony, you gave your hand into your husband's that ring was given a new meaning as the Sign of the Cross confirmed and consecrated your love. The greatness of Christ, love on a cross, made your love into a sacrament. And sanctified love makes marriage magnificent. Listen to Pope Pius XI in his encyclical on marriage, "Hence this Sacrament not only increases sanctifying grace, the permanent principle of the supernatural life . . . but also adds particular gifts, dispositions, seeds of grace, by elevating and perfecting the natural powers. By these gifts the parties are assisted not only in understanding but in knowing intimately, in adhering firmly, in willing effectively, and in successfully putting into practice those things which pertain to the marriage state, its aims and duties, giving them in fine the right to the actual assistance of grace whensoever they need it for fulfilling the duties of their state."

SAINTS IN APRONS brings into focus the sacramental basis of marriage. It is written from the inside. Rose Huesman, wife and mother, is an on-the-spot writer. The reflections presented here are drawn from life, from life real and rugged, joyful and painful, sinful and sacred. They bespeak an unusually keen power of observation that searches out the motives, the reasons why wives and mothers fail to put all they can into their married lives and hence fail also to bring into their homes all the happiness, all the power, all the beauty that sacred matrimony contains. If you are looking for simple solutions to your family problems put the book down now. But if you want to know more about yourself and more about the greatness of your vocation and the tremendous possibilities it offers you and how to get at them, then, this book is for you. These reflections are the product of prayerful soul-searching. They combine sound theology with good practical sense and that intuitive depth that manifest a wife's loving heart and a mother's deft hand.

Originally no wide audience was intended. The urge to put in writing what one felt so deeply within oneself gave birth to the first copy. Sickness, the needs of the children, family cares, and parish activities combined to push the manuscript off the kitchen table and into the catchall. For two years the reflections were left in darkness to reflect on themselves. It was the insistence of friends that brought them out of their solitude. No little prodding was necessary to get them into their present form. God helped make this possible by lessening the chores of the Huesman household. He Himself took over the care of three of the children. Their lives henceforth are for Him alone. Two sons are in the seminary. A daughter is a professed nun.

Do not be misled. This is not a book on vocations. It is on a *vocation* — the vocation of a wife and mother. Yet it is not too much to hope for that as more wives and mothers live out the principles it sets forth, more of our children will be given a divine calling.

Although primarily intended for wives and mothers, all those anxious about the sacredness of marriage and the holiness of the home will find it inspirational and instructive.

CASSIAN YUHAS, C.P.

INTRODUCTION

Coming from his vantage point in the sanctuary, a little altar boy once remarked to his mother: "Women are holier than men."

When asked how he had arrived at this conclusion, he answered: "There are always more women in church."

In looking at the picture of church attendance, reception of the sacraments, apostolic works, we may be inclined to form the same conclusion.

But are we really holier than our men? Does our spirituality have more depth and substance than the spirituality of our husbands and sons? We may like to think so; we may even point to the external proof that it is so. But if our holiness is as true and sincere and unshakeable as we like to believe it is, then the world, society, and family life would be feeling the strength of our holiness.

As it is, the world has never been in such a state of despairing conflict; society has never been so flagrantly attracted to vice, and the sanctity of family life has never been so seriously undermined. The man, woman, and children who live together in the holy bond of matrimonial love are becoming the exception rather than the rule.

The ideals of marriage have not changed. In fact the marriage ideal seems to be more lofty today than it has ever been. Yet more marriages are failing. And it is possible that more marriages are failing because we have become so enthralled with the marriage ideal that we are inclined to overlook the personal responsibility which helps cement the foundation of a happy marriage.

We hear so much of mutual responsibility, compatibility, equality, togetherness that we have actually allowed this ideal to become the excuse upon which we blame all our failures. Once the ideal of mutual compatibility becomes an excuse for failure it can no longer be the goal of marital perfection. It becomes instead a hardened wedge splitting marriage apart.

Of course there is supposed to be mutual responsibility and a harmonious kind of togetherness, for without them the goal of an ideal marriage would never be reached. However, all too often we expect marriage alone to supply the materials for the ideal we want, as though marriage were a kind of supply depot. We conveniently forget that marriage in itself can give us nothing except what we ourselves put into it. Before we can expect to reap the fruits of happiness and peace from marriage we must learn to shoulder every bit of personal responsibility which the vocation demands of us, as well as share the mutual responsibilities.

In marriage there are many mutual responsibilities. Both husband and wife are mutually responsible for each other's spiritual and temporal welfare, just as they are mutually responsible for the spiritual and temporal welfare of the children born of their union. This mutual responsibility, though, is supposed to be a positive thing — a harmonious working together for the benefit of all. It is not supposed to be a negative excuse for avoiding personal responsibility.

For example, a husband and wife know that it is their mutual responsibility to go to church and to see that the children attend. However, the husband does not bother about church nor is he concerned whether or not the children attend. Therefore, this being a *mutual* responsibility and one in which he will not co-operate, then she feels justified in dropping the responsibility also. What should have been mutual responsibility becomes instead mutual irresponsibility.

How many families have fallen into spiritual decline because of this negative approach to responsibility. Marriages are wrecked, homes are broken, and more and more delinquent children wander through life without purpose, direction, or goal.

That is why we should never lose sight of the importance of personal responsibilities. And they are those for which we alone, as individuals, will be held responsible. When we stand before the judgment seat of God He will not be judging the rest of the family. He will be judging us. And he will be judging us according to how we have assumed our personal responsibilities. If we have not been conscientious about our personal responsibilities, the mutual responsibilities of marriage are not likely to save us.

Our personal responsibilities as wives and mothers are more intimately and personally private and are more concerned with the state of our own soul, our personal relationship with God, with our husband, children, and all those with whom our lives are bound up.

Take our personal responsibility for the spiritual and temporal welfare of our spouse. Here is one particular responsibility about which we can become awfully confused. We are inclined to consider our husband's spiritual welfare in terms of a third-degree spotlight which we turn upon him to determine how often he prays or how often he receives the sacraments. We hardly ever stop to consider this responsibility with regard to ourselves — whether or not we are an occasion of sin to him.

A wife may have a vile temper, which of course she can't help and which of course her husband is supposed to suffer. If he can stand it long enough it may make a saint out of *him*, but it won't make a saint out of her!

This is not the way God intended that we help sanctify our husband — by making a martyr out of him. We are not supposed to inflict the practice of heroic charity upon him because we can never get around to controlling our temper. It is our personal responsibility to learn to control the temper that he might enjoy the blessing of a peaceful home.

The same holds for his temporal welfare. A lot of wives think that responsibility for their husbands' temporal welfare means goading them to make more and more money until they drop dead from overwork. Our personal responsibility here is keeping our husbands well and contented by letting them know that we can be content by managing the family budget allotted to us and stretching it to provide happiness and peace for all. Money doesn't make a happy home, but an appreciative and contented wife often does.

These are but a sampling of a wife's personal responsibilities which are so very important for the growth of her own personal holiness and for the increase of marital happiness.

It is in this personally private, spiritually interior, area that so many of us are failing. This failing has come about, not so much by willful rejection of the kind of virtue which leads to union with God, but by a mistaken understanding of what constitutes true virtue. Our preoccupation with externals has taken away the realization that personal virtue must have roots in the hidden recesses of the soul deriving nourishment and strength from the divine indwelling.

We are losing sight of this truth to the extent that we have actually come to believe that a well-kept house, a blemish-free complexion, a well-deodorized and beautifully clothed body constitute real virtue. If we are able to present a pleasing picture to all who see us, then we are judged virtuous — we become convinced we are virtuous.

But virtue is more than preoccupation with externals. We suspect it every time we have a quiet moment, for the restless rebellion of our soul reminds us that this is not why we were created; this is not why we became wives and mothers.

And the urge to run away from the lie we are living becomes so much of a compulsion that we are tempted to try anything as an escape. But we cannot escape a lie except by embracing the truth.

It is the truth with which these reflections are concerned. The plain, unadorned, sometimes painful, sometimes humiliating truth.

Because these reflections were written for the purpose of helping the wife and mother to grow in self-knowledge, many of these chapters are written in a very subjective manner which at times may seem painfully personal. This subjective style is intentional as it is used to help the reader more easily investigate the various barriers which human weakness sets up against the inflowing of God's grace. Other chapters are written in an instructional manner, depending upon the material covered.

In progressing through these *Reflections*, the reader will note that husbands are rarely mentioned, except in passing. This is also intentional, because there isn't a married woman alive who could not write a book about husbands.

And this is not a book about husbands. This is a book for wives and mothers. A book which could be considered as a kind of spiritual mirror which one might use for an objective glimpse into the soul — not the soul of the husband, not the soul of a child, but the soul of the wife and mother.

THE AUTHOR

CONTENTS

SAINTS IN APRONS

REFLECTIONS ON CONJUGAL LOVE

In my bed by night I sought him whom my soul loveth: I sought him and I found him not.

I will rise and go about the city: in the streets and in the broad ways I will seek him whom my soul loveth. I sought him and I found him not (Cant. 3:1–2).

RESTLESS NIGHT

Your husband may be sleeping peacefully beside you, but a core of restlessness within you flares into spiritual heartburn. You have the strange feeling that, although you are sure you have been given bread, in reality you have devoured a stone.

What has happened? Nothing unusual really, except a stirring inherent spiritual instinct which knows that the flesh alone can never supply what the spirit seeks. Not even in marriage. Not even in a marriage which carries with it God's blessing in the sacramental union.

No matter how much in love we were at the time of marriage; no matter how high our ideals were concerning marriage; no matter how blissful our marital union has seemed to be, the restlessness will come and will either undermine our conjugal love or will solidify it in God, depending upon our efforts. This restlessness is spiritual and it will never be assuaged until it is put to rest in God. And it is important for us to realize

1

this, otherwise we shall wander about the city and the broad ways the rest of our lives never ever finding the One whom we seek.

Without a true understanding, this restlessness may take over, manifesting itself in any number of ways. The virtuous, considering the condition a temptation against marriage vows, may repress it as completely as they can, then, resting in the virtue of such repression, wind up neurotic old women no good to themselves or anyone else.

Those who disregard the spiritual component in human nature and relegate this restlessness to a carnal seeking of the all will invariably begin to wander. For them carnal union must be complete union so they discard one marital partner after another, convinced that the individual selected to provide such union has somehow failed. These souls are to be pitied. In them the hope of finding him whom they seek flares so long as they live, then smolders out in despair when they die.

Then there are those who accept this restlessness as a challenge and who do their seeking in the determination to conquer the world. They try careers, or they paint abstract pictures or write silly novels. Or perhaps they try to lose themselves in worthy causes: organizing organizations, making speeches, and trying to reform everyone they meet.

Do not misunderstand! There is nothing wrong with hobbies or with activities which are kept in their rightful place. Paint an abstract picture if you must — or write a novel — or sign up for some worthy cause. Just be sure that these activities are being done for the enjoyment, relaxation, and good they will do you and others, and that your talents are not being used as an escape from the reality of marriage. There is no escape from this reality, for the reality of marriage is God.

How blind, how deluded can we be? This restlessness is merely the caressing finger of God, placed upon our hearts to stir in them the flame of His divine love. He wants us for Himself. We respond to His invitation by seeking Him in everything else except what He is and in every place else except where He is. We may glimpse Him momentarily in all the things we substitute for Him, but we will never find Him completely in any of them.

God can be found only where that core of restlessness starts — in the center of the soul.

PARADISE OR PARADOX

Marriage is a paradox only inasmuch as we are convinced that marriage is paradise. And those who marry expecting, from that day forward, to take up an abode in an earthly paradise are in for a rude shock. The privilege of living in an earthly paradise was taken away from humanity with the commission of original sin.

When Adam and Eve were put out of Paradise, they were already married. Marriage was in no sense a substitute paradise given to them by God as an afterthought, a kind of shifting from one kind of paradise to another or from one level of bliss to another.

God did not say to our first parents, "Go from this paradise, but in your conjugal love you will find a paradise which is equal, if not superior to this one."

What God actually said, as recorded in Genesis, was (to Eve): "I will multiply thy sorrows, and thy conceptions. In sorrow shalt thou bring forth children, and thou shalt be under thy husband's power and he shall have dominion over thee."

And to Adam: " '. . . cursed is the earth in thy work; with labor and toil shalt thou eat all the days of thy life. . . . In the sweat of thy face shalt thou eat bread till thou return to the earth out of which thou wast taken: for dust thou art and unto dust thou shalt return.' And the Lord God sent him out of the paradise of pleasure to till the earth from which he was taken" (Gen. 3:16–23).

With the commission of sin the security, the happiness, the

untroubled joy of living in an earthly paradise was lost to humanity forever. Paradise is gone from the earth, but the nostalgia for such an abode has never been uprooted from the human heart.

For those who do not believe, or do not care to heed, the truth that paradise has been re-established for us in eternity by Jesus Christ, life is one futile search. Over the years every corner of the earth has been searched; every mode of human existence has been analyzed; not a stone has been left unturned by those looking for a clue which will lead to the rediscovery of Paradise Lost. But the earth, and the things of the earth, and the people of the earth have never divulged the secret of its whereabouts because paradise is not found in any of these things.

But the searchers, who can never reconcile themselves to defeat, go on searching. Not having found paradise — for that reality eludes them — they have settled for a substitute; the best substitute they could find: *romantic love.* They have not found paradise, they have found only its forbidden fruit.

Eating of the forbidden fruit condemned Adam and Eve, but to those who would capitalize upon their discovery, you would think that a diet of forbidden fruit is the only diet which could assure the healthy vigor of happiness in this world.

"Eat of this fruit," they would seem to say, "gorge yourself upon it, the more you become sated with it the closer you will come to paradise, for paradise is not a reality it is only a state and you will find it only in the abandonment of romantic love."

We may not believe this, but the atmosphere in which we live has become so hazy with this heresy that it is almost impossible not to breathe some of it and consequently to be affected by it. As Catholic wives and mothers we probably have the conviction that it isn't true, but such a conviction does not always bring joy. We see the infection spreading among the young, undermining the spiritual aspect of marriage; we find it all too often undermining the foundation of our own marriages.

In anticipation romantic love may appear as the doorway to paradise, but we know from experience that romantic love is not paradise. The pleasure inherent in romantic love is only a transient thing, poised momentarily in time and at its best only a fleeting taste of the pure bliss for which we go on searching all our lives.

Expect romantic love, culminating in sexual abandonment (in marriage or outside of marriage) to be paradise and we will be worse than disappointed. We will feel cheated, exploited, contaminated.

Instead of finding the paradise of bliss we expected of marriage, we find only the paradox of suffering and discontent.

UNION OR HARMONY

One of the most monstrous fallacies to be born from this preoccupation with sex wearing the halo of romanticism is that this romantic state somehow fuses the "essence" of two mortals into some kind of divine being: one in body, one in mind, one in soul.

Of course the sacramental union of marriage is real and binding and those who marry do become two in one flesh. But they do not become two in one will, two in one intellect, two in one spirit. Such union is not a human prerogative; it is only the divine prerogative. Such union exists only in the Blessed Trinity; it can never exist between two human beings no matter how much they may love each other — romantically or otherwise.

As human creatures, we must always be separated from those we love by reason of our human limitations. There are no two human beings in the whole world who have precisely the same thought at precisely the same time, nor the same degree of understanding of the same idea, nor the same comprehensive knowledge about the same things. We are all united in our human nature and love may unite us in smoother harmony, but we must always conform to the limitations which separate us one from another.

It is perfectly natural for the human creature to seek union with the beloved, and to believe that union in conjugal love is perfect union in perfect love. The kind of love which propels men and women into each other's arms — and consequently into marriage — would seem to promise fulfillment of the soul's desire for this kind of perfect union. But this is only an illusion.

Even in being united with the one we love, we must still depend upon words for communicating; we must still remain at the mercy of another's understanding of our deepest emotions. We may share our joys, our sorrows, our disappointments, our ambitions, our frustrations, but we cannot project any of these things into another's mind simply by willing them there.

It usually does not take long for the newly married to emerge from the illusion that the marriage ceremony did not fulfill the perfect union it seemed to promise at the time. It does not take too long to realize that a silence can be mistaken for moodiness, or that a word can be misconstrued and cause an argument.

By the time the haze of illusion clears away revealing the harsh reality of human limitations, we can hardly be blamed for wondering if, somehow, we have been cheated; for wondering how we could have been so lost in this illusion of so-called perfect union when there seems to be no real — at least no tangible — union at all.

Except in the physical. In this physical union this illusion begins; here it must also end.

The day we recognize this illusion for what it is: part of God's plan to unite us in marriage with the one we love, then this is the day of our maturity. This is the day of fostering the loving harmony which will bridge the gap of human limitations. Then we will learn to accept our marital union as it is, with all its limitations, and not as we dreamed it might be: bliss without end and life without vicissitude.

LOVE'S DUAL GUISE

Falling in love doesn't usually throw us into the state of confusion. We may become absent-minded, but never confused. Falling in love sets up an irresistible goal for us: marriage. It is only after we are married that we are likely to become confused.

Our goal seems to be behind us instead of ahead of us. Living the marriage vocation seems an anticlimax to the anticipation of the marriage ceremony. The goal during courtship was marriage and love fulfilled. The goal after marriage too often bogs down to one great big question mark.

Our confusion is likely to stem from the fact that, as wives and mothers, our vocation offers love to us in two guises: the human and the divine; the carnal and the spiritual. That our vocation gives us the privilege of exercising both these loves on both their most exalted planes should be a source of consolation to us, not a source of confusion. These two loves should be balanced in perfect harmony in our lives. Our confusion starts when we try to separate the two.

And we do tend to separate them, inadvertently perhaps, but we do. Loving our husbands and our children seems to take all we have to give of this particular emotion. Loving God comes off second best. We may love God inasmuch as we try to keep the rules, but we are not inclined to love Him with the passionate abandon with which we love a lot of other people — and things. That kind of love, we presume, is for those in the religious life. Our love at its best tends to stay on the human or natural level, and in keeping it there we fail to realize that love, consistently practiced on such a level tends to degenerate.

Although the honeymoon atmosphere may have its delights, this is not the apex of human love despite what is said or implied by those who would have us believe that it is. It is only in the atmosphere of divine love that the human soul can reach the pinnacle of love here upon earth. Only in loving God above all things and knowing that this supernatural love is sanctifying our relationship with others, does human love come anywhere near perfection.

Christ Himself has told us: "Thou shalt love the Lord thy God with thy whole heart, and with thy whole soul and with thy whole mind. This is the greatest and the first commandment. And the second is like it, Thou shalt love thy neighbor as thyself" (Mt. 22:36–38). Christ did not separate human love from divine love and neither should we. His words apply to us who are married just as they apply to anyone else seeking sanctification in any other vocation.

It is worse than a pity that the general concept of marriage has degenerated into a materialistic, paganistic state in life in which everything else is important except the soul's — and the family's — spiritual welfare. "Loving God" has become something which seems to be the unique privilege of the religious, or some kind of substitute — a kind of straw grasped by those whose marriages have failed, or who have become widows, or who have been frustrated in loving on the human level.

The line of demarcation would seem to be drawn so definitely between those who love on the sense level and those who love on the spiritual level that it is hardly a wonder that we do become confused. In this confusion it would almost seem that the married are placed in a kind of spiritual ghetto, to eke out their spiritual sustenance as best they can, and if they escape this ghetto in their search for God it is not because of their marriage vocation, but despite it.

Although it is true that the vocation to the religious life is the more perfect vocation, it is equally true that those who enter the religious life do not have a monopoly upon sanctity. Sanctity becomes our birthright the day we are baptized and each individual's degree of holiness depends upon the use of vocational graces given by God rather than upon the vocation itself. A vocation in itself is only an external circumstance and will do nothing at all for us unless we utilize the wealth hidden in the graces which go along with it.

There are many excellent books written on the progress of the human soul toward God, but most of these books hardly do more for the married than to leave in them the feeling of futility. The aesthetic ideals set forth seem to be too far above us. And what is even more disappointing, these ideals are always (it seems) slanted toward those who have a more exalted vocation than ours.

One can study about the sublime heights to which prayer, silence, and solitude can raise the soul. One can ponder the beautiful realm of the spiritual life as the mystics portray it for us. One can desperately long to be included in the apparently "chosen few" who have "tasted and found that the Lord is sweet." But for all too many of the married this seems too much of a spiritual luxury to be reconciled with the reality of the marriage vocation.

But God *is* the reality of the marriage vocation. In order to find Him in our vocation our conjugal love must be what God intended it to be for us: a love which, while finding its expression on the physical or human level, must nevertheless be kept at all times on the spiritual — the divine — level. After all, the love God has given us to practice in marriage is only a reflection of His divine love and it must be exercised in Him or it will fail.

It will fail in our marriage, for pleasure can never supplant obligation. It will fail in our relationship with our husband and our children, for the pleasure of physical union can never be stretched to eliminate the trials and tribulations of the marriage vocation. It will fail most of all as the channel of grace that will propel us toward God and eternal salvation.

Human love in our lives separated from the divine is like an empty cup for the thirsty. The human heart can never find the fulfillment of love in another human being by keeping love confined to the human level, but the human soul *can* find the most perfect reflection of love that life has to offer in keeping the soul balanced in the perfect harmony of human and divine love in the vocation which is ours as wives and mothers.

But like everything else worth having, this harmonious love will never be ours unless we seek it. We sought the fulfillment of love in the anticipation of marriage. It may be that we feel, somehow, that marriage has not come up to our expectations. If this is true, then it is time for us to seek the love which will provide the missing element in our marriage; that in starting on our journey toward God in earnest, our marriage will become the fruitful vocation God intended it to be, bearing the fruits of love and joy and peace and spiritual security.

REFLECTIONS ON THE MASS

May God grant that (the laity) participate even every day, if possible, in the divine Sacrifice, not only in a spiritual manner, but also by reception of the august sacrament, receiving the body of Jesus Christ which has been offered for all to the eternal Father. . . . Let husbands and wives approach the holy table so that nourished on this food they may learn to make the children entrusted to them conformed to the mind and heart of Jesus Christ (Pius XII, Mediator Dei, November 20, 1947, n. 119).

THE CENTER OF OUR LIFE

The center of our life is marriage and the center of our marriage is Christ. In the course of our Catholic lives every sacrament we receive cements us more firmly and more perfectly into that Body which has Christ as its Head.

Marriage then is the crowning sacrament for us — wives and mothers. By our nuptial vows we bind ourselves not only to our husband, but also to God; we settle ourselves into our vocation which in turn is settled in God.

With every sacrament there are given particular graces which will increase our holiness in this life and assure our eternal salvation. Marriage is no exception. The sacramental graces inherent in matrimony are sufficient, not only to assure our salvation, but to raise us during our married life to an intimate union with God.

When we marry then, it is as though our heavenly Father

11

starts us off with an inexhaustible spiritual bank account, to be drawn upon and utilized as we need it. But like any other bank account, it will not become a means to any end unless it *is* drawn upon and utilized. We cannot buy a home for ourselves unless we use the family income for this purpose and neither can we buy an eternal residence in heaven unless we utilize the spiritual income which has been given to us. The spiritual treasury which is ours by right of the sacramental graces of matrimony will do us no good if we leave it lying unused by way of neglect or if we dissipate it by way of sin.

This is the fundamental truth concerning the sacramental graces of matrimony. The only trouble is that there are those who become so carried away by this fundamental truth that they cannot, or will not, see any farther. Resting complacently upon this fundamental truth is like living in the foundation of an incompleted house. So you have a good foundation! But a house needs more than a foundation before it can be enjoyed as a home. The money put into a safe deposit box will not become a home either unless we go get the money and use it for all the necessary things which go into the building of a home.

And so it is with our sacramental graces. We must go to the safe deposit box to get them. Our spiritual safe deposit box is kept and guarded for us in the Church. The key which has been given to us that we might exploit this treasure for all its spiritual worth is the Mass.

Here it comes, you may be thinking, here is someone who is going to tell me now that the only way I can be a good wife and mother is by running to church all the time! You may begin to argue that frequent attendance at Mass is not necessary; that it has been repeatedly pointed out to you that it is not necessary; that the very nature of the marriage vocation and its obligations prevent you from running to church every time the bell rings. Besides, you have been told often enough that God can be found in the home as well as in church!

This is also the truth; but only partly the truth. As wives and mothers we do not have to be "running to church all the time." We can thank God that we are not obligated under sin to make daily trips to the church. If we were under such an obligation we would be more wretched spiritual specimens than we are! What we should remember though, is that the duties and obligations which may excuse us from participating in the Holy Sacrifice of the Mass do not excuse us from appreciating what the Mass means to us. Unless we appreciate God's sacramental presence in the Mass, we are very likely to remain oblivious to His presence in our home.

The Mass is the center of our sacramental life. The Mass gives us Christ, the Center of our vocation. The two cannot be separated. If we try to separate one from the other, we are no longer fixed centrally in Christ. Our lives become off center.

OFF-CENTER LIVES

Of course you have gone to Midnight Mass at Christmas many times, but have you ever gone to early Mass the day after Christmas? The contrast in attendance is shocking to say the least! Church is just the same; the Mass is just the same; the Infant is still in His manger, but the church is quiet and empty.

We come in droves on Christmas Eve. We lose ourselves in dewy-eyed sentimentality over welcoming this adorable Infant who means so much to us — on Christmas Eve. On the day after Christmas we do not think it necessary to return in order to offer that same adorable Infant an extra token of love and gratitude!

We prefer to rest upon the premise that daily Mass is not really necessary for us; that God, for us who are married, can be found in the home.

Light can be found in the home too, also water — if we flick the light switches and turn on the faucets. Cut off light and water from their central source of supply though, and what do you have? Unresponsive light switches and water faucets.

The point to be made is this: the Mass is the central source of our sacramental life of grace. If we cut ourselves off from this central source of grace, we are not likely to find an abundance of grace in our homes. We cut off the living stream of grace channeled in our direction, for the Mass was instituted by Christ as the way in which He would remain with us — the Center — the very Heartbeat of our spiritual life.

If we happen to be among those who consider the Mass as nothing more than an external form of worship which obligates us on Sundays and holydays; or if we consider Mass as a spiritual luxury to be "enjoyed" by a few who have nothing else to do, then it is very possible that we are among those who are living off-center lives. And if we are living such off-center lives it is not our circumstances which need scrutinizing so much as our spiritual dispositions.

If our appreciation for the Mass is what it should be, then circumstances will not forbid our participation. True, this participation while we are tied down with small children may have to be mostly spiritual, but it will be effective. On the other hand, if our appreciation of the Mass is less than it should be then, no matter what our circumstances, we shall continue to use them as excuses for rejecting the spiritual treasure which is ours either by spiritual or active participation in the Mass.

And so, if the idea of daily Mass does not attract us, then the thought of God's presence in our home does not attract us either. We will not go to daily — or frequent — Mass for a number of reasons, and we will not find God in our homes either — usually for the same reasons, the most well worn of which are that we work and that there is too much activity in our home. And, stemming from these two reasons, other excuses increase and multiply in almost endless variety.

Reason Number One. We do not go to daily Mass because we work outside the home. Paradoxically, why we work usually determines whether or not we appreciate the necessity for frequent or even daily attendance at Mass; for those who work fall into one of two groups: those who work because of a necessity and those who work because they "have to."

Those of the first group are working for the only valid reason a wife or mother has for working outside the home: to supplement or provide a *necessary* or truly useful income for her family. Prompted by a husband's unemployment, illness, or irresponsibility, she works solely for the purpose of providing the basic needs of the family. Within this group are found a high percentage of daily Communicants. They have long ago found that the Mass and Holy Eucharist provide the spiritual stamina they need in order to keep going in the face of adverse circumstances. Wives and mothers in this group are living Christ-centered lives and are usually a source of admiration and edification for everyone.

But there are all too many who fall into the second group: those who work because they "have to." Why we "have to" work outside the home can cover a lot of ground, but it can be boiled down to two fundamental reasons: because we are greedy for material things or because we use working as a means of escaping our marital responsibilities.

If we find ourselves among this group, then we are also likely to be numbered among those who consider Mass as a spiritual luxury in which we cannot afford to indulge. And right we are! We cannot afford indulgence in the things of God if we are convinced that the things of the world mean more to us. If we can manage to sandwich a Sunday Mass into our busy week we feel we are being very generous with God. That is enough! If we give Him any more than that, He may take away everything for which we have worked so hard!

Our lives are woven, tied, and strangled with excuses. We may have married with good intentions, but they have long since become the good intentions lightly spoken of as those which pave the road to hell. And we have so many *good* reasons for working! Most important is that the added income will make our marriage more successful. But has it? Our marriage has become an empty cart into which we pile every material thing we can grasp. And then, wielding the double-thonged whip of ambition and greed, we sit on top, giving the horses of our passions full reign to dash headlong wherever their whims and instincts carry them.

Or we may work because we hate the boredom and monotony of housework; yet we want a beautiful home which we can display with pride and joy. So we spend every waking moment working for the salary which keeps our home so beautiful that we are never able to enjoy it!

Or we may work because we have a lot of obligations, which are all neatly itemized — with all the important things first. Items such as a new car, smart clothes, entertainment, imported knickknacks. There is no room on the list for an obligation itemized as maternal. We ignore it whether we have acquired it or not. If there are children, we relegate their haphazard care to others. If there are none we congratulate ourselves upon our good fortune.

A remark that even remotely suggests that God can be found in the home strikes us with the same incongruity as does the statement that woman's place is in the home. And we toss off both these ideas with about the same facility with which we have learned to toss down the third cocktail at an office party. And with just about the same effect — we are left hilarious! Whose place is in the home? The cleaning woman's. The baby-sitter's. But never again ours. We have beaten ourselves a path and we are running it frantically. Our middle name is Career and we have become efficient, intellectual, and brittle.

God can be found in our home? Hardly. If He could be found there; if He manifested Himself visibly, we would not be there to see.

Reason Number Two. We do not participate in the spiritual benefits of daily Mass because there is too much morning activity in the home. This is a good excuse — the best one we can find and it can cost us not only our sanctity but our sanity as well if we are not careful.

Our husband may be a saint, but our lives have become off center because we resent the burden *his* virtue has placed upon us. He may appreciate our fruitful motherhood, but we do not. We could do with a little less virtue and a little more diversion. We cannot share his love and resignation to the will of God because it is a constant thwarting of our own will.

True, we married with good intentions. Conscientiously we have tried to assume our conjugal and maternal obligations, yet the more these obligations have increased the more our dissatisfaction, frustration, and complaints have also increased. We have become so exasperated with trying to keep God's laws that we suffer only the burden and the yoke. His sweetness and light never seem to be ours.

We presume God is in our home, or at least He is supposed to be there, for our husband reminds us often enough. But we can never find Him in the endless feeding of hungry mouths, washing of dirty faces, wiping of runny noses. In the cooking, cleaning, washing, ironing.

Our days have become punctuated with impatience and our love has become punctured with discontent. We see ourselves only as unappreciated drudges with no time for anything worthwhile. We have no decent clothes, our hair is a mess, our figure is gone. . . .

Where is God? We pray to Him often enough in sheer desperation, but we cannot find Him in our home. We cannot even find Him in our heart.

The above is an example of a wife and a mother who has a tremendous spiritual treasure and which could be increased even more by her spiritual participation in the Masses her husband attends so faithfully. Instead she resents the fact that his well-worn missal is only a symbol of the threadbare drabness of her home — her life.

She has every reason to be happy. Instead she has allowed selfishness and self-pity to distort her sense of values to the point where she can no longer see the dignity of her vocation as wife and mother, the beauty of motherhood, nor can she appreciate the blessing of a virtuous husband.

Off-center lives are unhappy lives. Preoccupation with material things — either the accumulation of them or the inordinate desire for them — is a poor substitute for the things of God.

Material things may seem more important than God's presence in our soul and in our home, but they cannot take His place. The more we insist upon centering our lives around them, the more spiritually withered and barren they become.

A GOOD HABIT

It does not matter really, why we have started to go to daily Mass, or how long we have been going. What matters is that we have started the daily Mass habit and despite all good reasons to the contrary, we have persevered. In common with every Catholic wife and mother the world over we share a lot of reasons why we may excuse ourselves from daily Mass. Instead we have worked at cultivating a good habit and have found a treasure. Such an exchange that is! Our miserable excuses for the infinite spiritual treasure of the Mass.

Now, after having become a daily Communicant, we are inclined to smile at those first, bleak, early morning ventures. That was hardship, we have to admit, and it was also a searing lesson in humility. We felt at first, that rendering this personal service to God we had climbed head and shoulders over everyone else. Our spiritual pride was painfully wounded with the discovery that most of our companions at daily Mass were attending also despite all the excuses we had rested upon for so long.

We have come to know them now, and to watch for them and see that they come to Mass morning after morning. Those wives and mothers who work; those who are expecting babies;

those who have small children, school children, working children; those whose husbands work odd shifts, whose husbands are ill; those who live at a distance; those who are infirm and crippled; those who are aged. We marvel at all these wonderful women who come to God and receive Him day after day.

And so we try now to go to daily Mass for it is a heavenly start for every wonderful day in our life. We know it every morning that we leave the sleeping house behind us. In the early morning silence our heart lifts to God as naturally as our eyes lift to the sky in a gesture of welcome for the new day.

On the way to Mass the new day is always a source of marvel for it is always beautiful; no matter what the season, no matter what the weather. The newborn beauty of the day is ours to enjoy in the spring when the sunrise sweeps the sky with shimmering color; in the summer when the cool dew sparkles wherever the risen sun finds it; in the autumn when glistening frost highlights the blaze of flaming leaves; in the winter's darkness when the morning star tells us the sun is not far away. We come to enjoy the fresh, clean splash of early morning rain; the crunch of our boots on untouched snow. Every morning on the way to early Mass is one of God's infinite surprises planned especially for us. No morning is ever drab or disappointing.

Our early morning tryst with God is an inconvenience to no one except ourselves, and even that inconvenience was canceled out the day we discovered that going to daily Mass had ceased being a hardship and had become a journey of love. We do not mind, any more, the hour's sleep we forego in order to be back home in time for the rest of the family's usual rising hour.

Our family benefits, too, from our early morning excursion. By the time we have returned home and started breakfast, we are wide awake and alert. We are fully dressed. We are enjoying the smell of the coffee perking and we are ready and able to handle the early morning hubbub which hungry and hurried families cause.

But more than this, we are serene and we are composed.

We are relishing Christ in our heart and we are delighting in His presence. We *know* now that God is in our home — with us even here in the kitchen — because we have brought Him home with us and put Him there. Everyone else knows it too. Everyone is more orderly and respectful around the mother who has just come from Holy Communion.

OUR SACRIFICE

"Pray, brethren, that my sacrifice and yours may be well pleasing to God the Father almighty" (*Orate Fratres*, Ordinary of the Mass).

The only ones who may profitably stay away from Mass are those who love the Mass so much that absence from it is a painful deprivation.

But how many of us can claim a place in that category? They are those who know that the Mass is our Sacrifice; not merely a private ritual carried out by a priest for our edification. They know that the Mass is not simply an external form of worship the attendance at which discharges a duty of obligation; and that it is not a spiritual luxury to be enjoyed by an enviable few. They know that the Mass is none of these things. They know that the Mass is the very center of their lives.

Some of us may envy such souls, but we would do better if we stopped envying them and joined them! Whether we realize it or not, the Mass *is* the center of our lives. It is our Sacrifice. It is the perfect act of worship rendered to almighty God by Christ first on Calvary, and now always, in time, by His Mystical Body.

And we are the Mystical Body of Christ. You and I and every Catholic who has ever been, or who ever will be, baptized. However, being incorporated into the Mystical Body does not necessarily perfect our individual participation in this Sacrifice. Before our participation can become a perfect part of the whole we must appreciate this Sacrifice for what it is worth, and participate as intelligently and as reverently as possible.

So you may argue that you do not understand the Mass; that because you do not fully understand it, you cannot become interested in it. It is too much of a mystery. Of course the Mass is a mystery — one of the mysteries of our faith — but is that a valid reason to remain indifferent to the Mass and thus deprive ourselves of its fruits?

All we have to do is look around us for that answer. Are all those who love the Mass intellectual giants? No. Many of the most ardent lovers of the Mass are those who have never been educated in much of anything, much less in the fine points of the Mass; yet they love it and appreciate it for all its spiritual worth.

Because the Mass is one of the mysteries of our faith, we obviously need more than an intellectual approach to any profitable understanding of it. An intellectual approach alone cannot penetrate into the divine Heart where the mysteries of our faith are hidden. The human intellect can go only so far; by reason of its limitations, it must stop. Only faith can bridge the gap between human ignorance and divine knowledge.

Such a faith has been given us in baptism and it is God's will that this faith should carry us to the very center of His heart — which is the Mass, there to be lost and to become one with Him who is both Victim and Priest.

This is God's will for us, but unfortunately it is not always our will. And because our will is not conformed to God's we miss out on the most marvelous, the most wonderful, the most spiritually fruitful Gift that God offers us in this life. We miss out on it. When all that is needed on our part is to want it; to will, along with God, that our own participation in the Holy Sacrifice be as perfect as possible for us and thus become a valuable contribution to the perfection of the whole Mystical Body.

Our first concern, then, must be how we can become as far

as possible a perfect part of this Holy Sacrifice; of this whole unity and union which is established between God and the faithful by means of the Mass.

Like everything else God plans for our welfare, the fruits of the Mass have already been established for us. They are there for us to enjoy and to utilize; but they will not be forced upon us against our will. God has already done the most important part for us. There remains, then, our part; and our part consists primarily of three things: disposition, participation, and appreciation.

In explaining this let us suppose that a king had invited us to his banquet. We receive his invitation in one of three ways: we are overjoyed, we are indifferent, or we ignore it altogether. Suppose, though, that we are overjoyed and so our acceptance begins with activity. We begin planning what we shall wear, how we shall act, and so on. We choose our gown and accessories with great care, not only because we want to appear beautiful in the king's sight, but because attention to personal detail is one way we have of showing how much we appreciate the honor which has been bestowed upon us.

On the day of the banquet, we prepare ourselves further for we not only desire to attend, we also desire to participate. We refrain from eating beforehand so that our appetite will be keen enough to appreciate all the delicacies we know the king will expect us to enjoy.

When the time for the banquet arrives we go and we participate; which means simply that we do what everyone else does. With the king and with the guests, we exchange friendly conversation, we eat, we drink, and we are all joined together in mutual enjoyment. The king has shown his love for us by preparing such a lavish feast; we have shown our love and appreciation for him by accepting his invitation and participating in it.

This is how we should consider the invitation to come to Mass. Our disposition, participation, and appreciation should be much the same except for the realization that no earthly king could ever provide a banquet which could compare with the Eucharistic Banquet which God has prepared for us.

In this light, let us consider disposition again. In regards to the Mass this will comprise two important elements: preparation and desire.

The preparation is much the same, but it is interior rather than external. The only gown which will impress our Eucharistic King is the garment of sanctifying grace. So if our "gown" has been ruined by mortal sin, we get a new one by means of a good confession. We give attention to personal detail by freeing ourselves as far as possible from venial sin and all attachment to sin.

As for stimulating our desire, we refrain from everything which would dull our spiritual appetite for the heavenly Food which is to be served to us. We do this not only by abstaining from food and drink for the required time, but also by mortifying our sensual desires and appetites.

And then we go to Mass and we participate. Which means again simply, that we do what everyone else is doing. With the priest, we enter into the Sacrificial Banquet with reverence, attention, and appreciation. We partake of the divine Food which is offered to us by the King Himself, we accept it gratefully, and we utilize it by allowing Christ to conform our souls more and more unto His likeness.

This, in simple form, is our part in the Holy Sacrifice. It doesn't seem like very much. It is not much in a sense, especially when we consider our nothingness. Considering ourselves as we really are, sinful creatures, not worthy even to be found in God's sight, we would have to admit that our attendance at Mass could mean absolutely nothing. Our presence there could be without any meaning or value at all; valueless in God's sight and valueless so far as ourselves or others are concerned.

But thanks to the goodness of our heavenly Father it is not that way at all. We have become infinitely precious in His sight, and our participation in the Mass is infinitely valuable. And why? Because when He looks upon us, God looks upon Christ, His beloved Son who shared our humanity in order that we might share His divinity.

We became one with Him in His Sacrifice on Calvary; He remains one with us in His Mystical Body. When Christ's Sacred Heart was pierced with a lance on Calvary it was not the end for us; it was the beginning. For at that moment we were born in Him. At that moment Christ's perfect Sacrifice was at once consummated, and we were at once drawn into the Heart of that Sacrifice to continue it *in Him* until the end of time. Our participation in the Mass, then, is just our active participation in the only Sacrifice which is perfectly pleasing to almighty God.

What a joy and a consolation this should be for us! Christ could have left us an actual, bloody crucifixion as an inheritance. But He did not. He left us the unbloody Sacrifice of the Mass. He could have made our salvation dependent upon the same cruel instruments of torture that were used to mutilate His innocent body. But He did not. He knew that we were too weak to join Him in such a sacrifice. Instead, He took our weakness upon Himself in order that He might give us His strength.

It is in the Mass that we are able to render to God the only act of worship which is perfectly pleasing to Him. We worship, not on our own, but with, in, and through Christ. By reason of our baptism we are incorporated into His Body, and being a member of His Body we share in His priesthood. The divine office of Christ's priesthood was perfectly fulfilled in His Sacrifice on Calvary; the office of His priesthood which we share finds its perfect expression in the Sacrifice of the Mass.

Entering into this Sacrifice, we accept the invitation from our King to come to the Eucharistic Banquet. We come to Him bringing nothing but ourselves and (let us hope) our good dispositions. We offer there poor gifts to Him in the form of bread and wine. As such they have little value, but that is all we have to give. At the Consecration the offering is endowed with infinite value for it becomes Christ, our Head, offering Himself with us, the rest of His Body, to God our Father.

The offering is infinitely pleasing to God. He accepts our gift and in exchange He gives us His Gift: Christ in Holy Communion. Christ's Sacrifice and ours is complete.

"May the homage of my service be pleasing to You most Holy Trinity, and grant that the sacrifice which I, all unworthy, have offered up in the sight of Your majesty, may be acceptable to You, and, through Your mercy, obtain forgiveness for me and for all those for whom I have offered it. Through Christ our Lord. Amen" (Ordinary of the Mass).

THE DIVINE LOVE SONG

Through the liturgy we become part of the voice of the Mystical Body, singing the perfect praise which only the Church can sing and which alone is perfectly pleasing to God. As the scroll of the liturgy unwinds over the seasons of the Church Year, we find in it everything we need to know and practice that our lives may become harmonized with Christ and more fruitful in Him.

During Advent we voice our petitions for the coming Emmanuel in the words of the prophets and the psalmists and thus we begin a conscious spiritual preparation for the feast of Christ's Nativity. The liturgical theme of preparation sung during Advent causes us to meditate and reflect upon the true meaning of Christmas. We learn to rejoice that the Light, which had for so long remained hidden from a darkened world, is ours to appreciate and to cherish. And even as we join the ancient prophets in the petition for the long-awaited Redeemer, we relish, from our own maternal experience, the anticipation of Mary as she makes her loving preparations for the Babe who will soon be resting in her arms.

What joy is ours when we open our missal to the Christmas

Mass and find the words: "The Lord said to me, You are my Son; this day have I begotten You" (Ps. 2:1). We know that the Infant Savior, the Son of God, is born in us and that we are all born again in Him. We anticipate the coming of His Real Presence in the Consecration of Midnight Mass and His actual coming to us in Holy Communion.

We prepare for Him a manger in our heart which of necessity must be filled with the straw of our weakness and sinfulness but a heart generous nevertheless, and glowing with the warmth of our poor welcome. We receive Him and we adore Him. We are at once the poor shepherds receiving His peace and the wealthy Magi filled with His substance. He is ours and we are His!

On Ash Wednesday we become mindful of the force and the ascendancy of the powers of darkness which would presume to engulf and annihilate even the Son of God. We accept the Church's invitation to flee this danger which would destroy us also; and take refuge in the penitential discipline she now so lovingly and wisely imposes upon us for the forty days of Lent. Fortified by daily Mass and Holy Communion, we day by day receive the spiritual strength to mortify our concupiscent appetites.

From our missals we pray with the Church that our fasting and penances may be pleasing to God and "profitable to us as a healing remedy." We learn that we are not to fast "as the hypocrites, sad. For they disfigure their faces, that they may appear unto men to fast. . . . But . . . anoint thy head and wash thy face; that thou appear not to men to fast, but to thy Father who is in secret: and thy Father who seeth in secret will repay thee" (Gospel of Ash Wednesday). We learn to fast as we should, joyfully and generously. And while we may suffer physical hunger, we learn that hunger suffered for Christ keeps us ever mindful of Him and of His Sacred Passion. It enkindles within us the desire to share that Passion with Him.

Through the daily liturgy of Lent we watch the drama of Christ's Passion unfold. We stand as horrified witnesses to man's insidious treachery which culminated in the crucifixion and death of the innocent Lamb of God. As the days of Lent progress we are caught up in the rumbling, surging mob hysteria which is stilled only with the spilling of the last drop of Precious Blood. We sorrow with Christ and taste the loneliness which was His upon being deserted by His chosen friends. We gaze with piercing sorrow upon the gaping wounds left by the scourge; by the dragging cross; by the jolting falls.

On Good Friday we kneel, numb with anguish at the foot of the cross, sorrowing with our Sorrowful Mother over this most infamous execution. As we contemplate the indescribable sufferings and shameful death of our Savior we come to realize that our presence at the Good Friday Mass of the Presanctified is not a mere commemoration of an event which took place over nineteen hundred years ago. It is an active participation in the Sacrifice of Calvary; that same Sacrifice consummated once upon Calvary's Hill, yet fixed immutably in time by the perpetual offering of the Holy Sacrifice of the Mass. That same Sacrifice which we have offered through the hands of the priest at daily Mass; the same immolation of the innocent Victim; shedding His blood in order to redeem those who have crucified Him by the same sins committed by the same sinners from the beginning to the end of time.

No longer can we indifferently shrug off the blame of Christ's crucifixion and death upon some thoughtless, malicious knot of humanity which perpetrated a crime, the thought of which shocks us once every year. On the contrary, we come to understand that as the Sacrifice of Calvary is a perpetual actuality, so is our participation in the Passion of Christ an actuality. It cannot be otherwise. We are either, by our indifference or our sins, guilty of constantly crucifying Him, or we are lovingly participating in His Redemption by suffering our own personal passion in union with His.

Our hearts echo Christ's anguish as we follow the Good Friday Liturgy: "O my people, what have I done to you, wherein have I afflicted you? Answer me." What answer can we give Him on this most sorrowful day except the silence of our reparation and our love.

On Holy Saturday night we share in a special way the joy of Mary Magdalen who was favored in hearing her name spoken by the risen Christ before the news of His Resurrection was known. Like her, we have experienced the emptiness of having been deprived of Christ's Real Presence. Coming into the darkened church and kneeling before the empty tabernacle gives us a vivid glimpse of Magdalen's desolation in finding the empty tomb, but unlike her we know that this dark emptiness will soon be filled with light. We glimpse the light first during the darkness of the Easter Vigil; we rejoice as it breaks forth in all its glorious splendor as the Resurrection Mass heralds the coming of the Risen Christ. The ringing bells and jubilant organ are no more joyful than our heart as it re-echoes the joyous *Alleluias* with which we sing of Christ's triumph over death.

Easter Sunday for us is truly "the day that the Lord hath made," and we are glad and we truly rejoice therein. Easter Sunday places the crown of triumph even upon us for through the liturgy and in union with all the other members of the Mystical Body we have shared Christ's Passion by mortification, prayer, and penance. We have participated in our Savior's Passion voluntarily and lovingly, so that now we may feast, "not with the old leaven, nor with the leaven of malice and wickedness; but with the unleavened bread of sincerity and truth" (1 Cor. 5:8). Our joy is beyond words for we are truly risen in Christ and rejoice in the newness of our life in Him.

As season follows season and the year progresses, the liturgy unfolds endless treasures of wisdom, understanding, and knowledge. Day after day it gives us familiar, yet ever new, glimpses of the Light which is Christ constantly shining in order to enlighten our darkness. The Light which is Christ in the voices of the Prophets of the Old Testament; the Light which is Christ in the New Testament. We find the same Light reflected in

His flawless Mirror: His most pure Mother; and we find the same Light shedding luster on all the saints whose names are included in the Church calendar. We come to know them all through the liturgy.

Through Masses sung in her honor we become more intimately acquainted with Mary Immaculate, Mother of God, Queen of heaven and earth. As the Church sings the sublime litany of her praises we come to love her more devotedly and to appreciate more thoroughly her peerless prerogatives. In the liturgy we find: "Glorious things are said of you, O Mary, for He who is mighty has done great things for you" (Communion, Mass of the Immaculate Conception). Each feast in honor of the Blessed Virgin which we celebrate along with the Church highlights another of these "glorious things" that are spoken concerning our heavenly Mother and draws us ever closer to her.

We also become better acquainted with all the saints through the Masses honoring their heroic sanctity. No longer do they seem to us mere holy-card faces backed with pious prayers, but friends and advocates. We recognize them as our spiritual brothers and sisters who have gone before us; heroes and heroines whose virtues we would aspire to imitate. They have triumphed over the same trials, temptations, and miseries which are ours in this life, and we know that there is hope that we may exchange these same things, as they did, for a heavenly reward.

In assisting at daily Mass we find, very often during the year, that the Requiem Mass starts our day. And so whenever the priest ascends the altar clothed in black we are prompted to offer with him sacrifice and prayers for the dead. By joining the priest in the Mass for the Dead we are reminded to pray not only for our own departed loved ones, but also for all of those who claim relationship with us in the Mystical Body.

The beautiful liturgy of the Requiem Mass is consoling and full of peaceful hope, for in it we find assurance that every soul touched by its benefits rejoices in eternal rest. In reading and reflecting upon the words of the Mass for the Dead we find that we meditate more often and more profitably upon our own death which is inevitable and for which are are reminded that we must be prepared. Familiarity with the Requiem Mass, along with reverent attention to the prayers and lessons contained in it help banish any fear and anxiety we may have concerning death.

In the Preface of this Mass we are given to understand: "For to your faithful, O Lord, life is changed, not taken away . . ." and we are consoled. We become more resigned to God's authority over life and death; our own life and death, and that of those dear to us.

OUR DAILY BREAD

Our heavenly Father expects us to ask for our daily bread; in fact we have been commanded by Christ to do so. We carry out this command of Christ most effectively by means of the Mass for in the Mass we beg God for our daily bread and through the Mass He grants our petition.

In the simple words *daily bread* there is hidden the essence of everything we need.

Stop a moment, and think what this *everything* means.

It means not only the food we need to nourish ourselves and our family; it also means the wherewithal to provide this food. So when we ask our heavenly Father for our daily bread in the Mass, He hears us begging trustfully for all of our temporal necessities; all the things we need to sustain us in this life.

These things are necessary for us in order that we maintain our allotted place in the Mystical Body. Our heavenly Father knows that these things are necessary for us and so His providential care of us is never stingy if we trustfully depend upon Him.

But over and above our temporal needs, He hears us begging for the spiritual Bread which He continues to give us in Christ, in the Eucharistic Bread. This is the most lavish of His gifts, the Remedy for all our ills, the strength of all our weaknesses, and the fulfillment of all our desires.

With our family's eternal welfare in mind then, along with our own spiritual advancement, can we really afford to forego the treasure which is ours in the Mass? We cannot if we want a share in all the good things which God has in store for us! Even if circumstances forbid our attendance at Mass, we should never let these circumstances prevent our spiritual participation in this divine Sacrifice. Once we come to appreciate the Mass and to love it, we will be drawn into it. God will draw us there and nothing, after that, will succeed in pulling us away.

If we already are daily Communicants, we can thank God for having given us the grace to draw closer to Him through the Mass and to beg Him further to teach us all we need to know in order to discharge faithfully the duties He has given us. If we have been bypassing daily Mass we should make a sincere effort to attend and beg God for the grace to persevere; so that in persevering our love for Him might increase, permeating the atmosphere of our home and keeping everyone mindful of His presence there.

The wife and mother who has a sincere love and appreciation for the Mass has a sincere love and appreciation for her home and for her family, and for her family's eternal welfare. The family reared and guided by the mother who is a daily Communicant is a spiritually wholesome, life-loving, responsible family; well equipped and capable of taking its place in the world; well equipped also for working for the whole good of society and for the honor and glory of God.

The children who have learned at an early age that Mass is part of their daily living, continually grow in the love and appreciation of their Catholic faith. Truth, chastity, and honesty are safeguarded in them and cherished by them as admirable traits of character. Grounded in Catholic ideals and principles, they tend to remain strong in their convictions and tend also to avoid anything which would try to destroy these convictions and ideals.

The home in which daily Mass begins the day is also the fruitful field from which religious vocations spring. Very often the boy who accompanies his parents to Mass is the son who "will go unto the Altar of God . . ." to celebrate the Mass he learned to love as a child. And the daughter who learned of the beauty of the Mass as a little girl may very well go on to be the bride of Him who gave Himself so often to her, that she might now become wholly His.

For all of us the Holy Sacrifice of the Mass is our life, our strength, our consolation in God. It is the most intimate and beneficial contact we can possibly have with Him in this life, for it is the sharing of His divine life. The Mass is by far the most precious treasure we may gather in this life and the one which we most assuredly may take along with us into eternity.

By participating in the Mass we most effectively carry out Christ's command to seek first the Kingdom of Heaven; and through the Mass all the other things are added to us, besides.

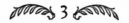 3

REFLECTIONS ON CONFESSION

To ensure more rapid progress day by day in the path of virtue, We will that the pious practice of frequent confession, which was introduced into the Church by the inspiration of the Holy Spirit, should be earnestly advocated. By it genuine self-knowledge is increased, Christian humility grows, bad habits are corrected, spiritual neglect and tepidity are resisted, the conscience is purified, the will strengthened, a salutary self-control is attained, and grace is increased in virtue of the sacrament itself (Pius XII, The Mystical Body of Christ).

CONFESSION

Confession is the anteroom to sanctity; the vestibule leading into the Interior Castle. If there is anything wrong with our confessions, there can never be anything altogether right about our spirituality.

The reason is simple. Unless we are truthful about ourselves with God, we set up a barrier against the inflowing of His grace. We may place the emphasis anywhere we please regarding the spiritual helps the Church offers, but unless we recognize ourselves as the sinners we are, none of these aids will do us much good. The efficacy of the Mass, the Holy Eucharist, prayer, all of the channels of grace upon which the soul relies for its spiritual nourishment are not entirely effective if we allow a confessional barrier to exist.

Unfortunately, such barriers may exist for any number of reasons — but they exist! And because they do exist confession becomes, for all too many Catholics, anything but the spiritual help it should be; anything from an indifferent habit to an insufferable torment.

How do these barriers come about? The answer to that one is simple, too. They begin the day on which we can't stand the thought of our vices, so we begin examining our consciences in the light of our questionable virtues. And the devil, who never fails to miss an opportunity, lends the helping hand that is needed — for his purpose. He paints such a magnificent picture of our virtues that our vices by contrast become minimized all the way down to nothing, or at least to insignificant importance. Hardly worth the bother of confession at all!

The baits the devil uses to trap the unwary soul into less effectual, or even untruthful, confessions, are various and assorted but the baits which seem to hold a peculiar attraction for women are those which we shall label self-justification, self-deception, scrupulosity, and oversensitiveness.

Since the same traps have been set with the same bait over and over we can't help wondering sometimes why we forever persist in reaching and falling, for most of us women are wary. We are also clever. And careful. We would never endanger our immortal souls by reaching for obvious sin. Obvious sin shocks us. It not only shocks us, it disgusts us.

The devil knows all this so he makes the bait attractive and because it is attractive we greedily reach for it — and fall.

SELF-JUSTIFICATION

Time for confession arrives. We start off to church feeling a little guilty over the sense of annoyance this obligation brings along with it. We remind ourselves that confession is supposed to be good for the soul. On the way to church we do a mental rundown of all the things we could be accomplishing if we didn't have to stop at this time for confession. We may even throw in an envious thought for Protestants.

The quiet semidarkness of the church soothes us a little; after a quick genuflection we kneel for a while in the presence of the Searcher of Hearts who is waiting to lift the burden from our souls.

Where do we begin . . . oh yes . . . O my God I am heartily sorry . . .

Conscience: For what?

We start with the Commandments. No adoring of idols — no disrespect for our parents — no missing Mass — no murder — no theft — adultery — all the way down the line. Nothing serious here.

Conscience: Then what?

We: Loss of temper.

Conscience: How many times?

Roughly figuring — number of days in month, etc.

We: About fifty times.

Conscience: Why?

We: Our mother-in-law (or husband, or children, or neighbor or any other person who may have had the misfortune to cross our path frequently and irritatingly during the past month)!

Conscience: What about these outbursts? Deliberate?

We relive them mentally.

Mother-in-law. Forever butting in — forever spoiling the children — forever making demands upon her son, just as though he were still her son and not our husband, forever being a constant and needling source of irritation with her unasked-for advice — her lack of respect for our privacy — her continual litany of ailments, mostly imaginary! A canonized saint couldn't be patient with such a mother-in-law. As a matter of fact, we might be a saint if it weren't for her — wouldn't have to go to confession at all, probably.

The outbursts begin to justify themselves until forty-nine of the fifty have been dissolved in the smoke of burning self-pity and self-righteous indignation.

We take the last remaining outburst into the confessional. After all we have to confess *something!*

Father listens while we tell him we have lost our temper, once.

And, Father, being no Curé of Ars who might look into our soul, accepts what we tell him and with the admonition to keep up the good work, gives us a short penance and absolution.

We emerge from the confessional feeling very pleased with ourselves, and very, very innocent. Why, Father must think we are a living saint! As we piously kneel to say our penance we are distracted by the upsurge of burning desire to do grandiose things for God. The vision takes hold and spreads. We become apostles spreading the faith. We become martyrs suffering the most cruel and bloody torments for the faith. We become . . .

Did Father say three or five Hail Mary's? We say five just to make sure we are being conscientious about our penance. We resolve to "keep up the good work."

Conscience: Which good work — maligning your mother-in-law or keeping your temper?

If we are smart we'll ignore that thrust.

We hurry home, confession already forgotten. We didn't see a very interested bystander who watched the whole proceeding with a diabolical grin on his face!

The conscience examination and confession given as an example might be amusing if it were not a case, too often, of being tragically true. And following it up, it does not take much stretch of the imagination to realize that this type of habitual self-justification might eventually lead to "justifiable" homicide. Justify a loss of temper this month and next month the temptation may be to justify a seething anger and before long a justified anger may grow into venomous hatred. Justified hatred not only can become damnation — it is damnation — hell begun on earth.

Trying to justify ourselves before God is useless. It amounts to nothing more than that we do an injustice to ourselves. We know that we cannot deceive God yet we stupidly persist in trying. We forget that, since He sees us always as we really are, self-justification is nothing more than a murky barrier of lies we use to try to hide the truth from His sight.

One sure way we can avoid the trap baited with self-justification is to examine ourselves objectively and sincerely.

Take mother-in-law again.

Instead of listing her sins, suppose we leave that personal affair to her. She goes to confession too, and has the privilege of telling her own sins to the priest.

We should ask ourselves rather:

Do we give her credit for having the same love and devotion for her son as we profess to have for our own children?

Do we respectfully listen to her advice — even if we do not follow it — or ask her advice on occasion?

Do we give her ample opportunity to enjoy her grandchildren, and do we teach them to love and reverence her as their father's mother?

Do we make her feel that she is a welcome guest in our home rather than an obnoxious intruder?

Do we extend little acts of kindness whether or not we think she appreciates them?

We may not like our mother-in-law but let us be truthful enough to admit that we are bound in charity and justice to extend to her the consideration and kindness owed her as a child of God. And let us be humble enough to resolve from this moment on to treat her as we hope to be treated when our own sons marry.

There is little room for self-justification in a truthful examination of conscience. In the light of truth we become ashamed of our outbursts, no matter in whose direction they may have been aimed — mother-in-law's or someone else's. If we have lost our temper fifty times, we will humbly admit as much in the confessional — without excuses — and come out disliking ourselves at the moment much more than we ever thought we could dislike the victims of our haranguing. Frequent repetition of these objective and truthful examinations of conscience and confessions will have many salutary effects. We will be surprised to find that most people aren't nearly so bad as we have made them, and as a result more fruitful friendships will develop. But even more important, we will grow in the active appreciation of what the sacramental grace of confession does for us and, in that appreciation, the barrier of self-justification will crumble, allowing us to move closer to God.

SELF-DECEPTION

Then there are those who persist in beating their spiritual heads against another kind of barrier! Twenty-nine days out of the month we are thoroughly convinced of our innocence. But the thirtieth day — confession day brings doubts and disquiet, for our innocence concerning involvement with a sin we avoid even thinking about (birth prevention) refuses to be backed with certitude. Examination of conscience becomes a process of elimination — elimination of guilt.

Our husband is adamant. He has all the children he wants or can afford. He is a non-Catholic (or a lax Catholic) and has no sympathy with the Church's stand on the subject. We must give generously of ourselves for the sake of conjugal peace and happiness. We hope the problem will be solved for us somehow, someday. We do not seem capable of solving it ourselves.

For one torturous moment we would be anyone or anywhere except who we are and where we are. We go into the confessional. We come out.

If we have done a thorough job of convincing ourselves of our innocence and our husband's guilt we have excused away any need for having discussed the problem with Father.

If, on the other hand, we have mentioned our predicament — all the while protesting our innocent involvement — and Father has told us in no uncertain terms what we are to do, we may leave the confessional too indignant and too proud to accept his reprimand and advice. And the promise Father extracted from us? It dies a quick death. It was given in exchange for the absolution we are certain we deserve. In our own eyes we are innocent again, for what else but innocence could be so crushed under Father's lack of sympathy and understanding?

And the conflict, far from being resolved goes on and on. Suppose Father's advice is heeded, what would happen? We would probably wind up with droves and droves of children — more than we could stand, much less support and care for. Or our husband, how would he react to the suggestion of voluntary continence? He can be very touchy when it comes to infringement upon *his* marital rights! He would probably turn to someone less virtuous. Then what would we do? How could we manage — and the children — how could we support them without out the help of their father? Isn't it better to run the risk of choosing the evil which appears the lesser when placed alongside of all these frightening possibilities? Suppose in standing firm we have only the questionable reward of seeing all that we have struggled for go crashing down around us.

All of these things may happen. And none of them may happen at all!

As wives and mothers, we enjoy believing that generosity is our prerogative and ours alone. We are reluctant to give anyone else, even our husbands, credit for sharing any of that virtue with us. We prefer believing that every other member of our household lives for the sole purpose of taking advantage of our generosity. We give and give and give. Everyone else merely takes.

What about our husband though? Here we are embroiled in a conflict, the reason for which as far as we can see, is our husband's selfishness and our own generosity. What other angles of the conflict, though, have we seriously considered?

Have we considered for example, that the reason for his obstinate stand may spring from the fact that he wants only to be generous with us? It could be that he is not entirely edified by our irritation and lack of patience with the children; that he chafes under the constant complaint that we are too tied down. It may be too that he grows morose over the realization that he simply cannot afford all the luxuries we forever remind him we need and his guilt may very well be the ointment of desperation he uses to try to soothe us. It could be the excuse he uses to keep from burdening us with the responsibility we have so positively indicated we do not want.

And it may very well be that someday the perversity with which we cloak our generosity will be all we have left to cover us; the only shield we have to use against the contempt and disgust which will have taken the place of the love and respect our husband once had for us.

Do we actually *know* what his reaction would be if we proved by our actions, that no matter how many children came along, we would welcome them as the fruit of our love? How would he react if he knew we are really happy and contented with what he is able to provide — how little or how much — so long as we are all united in the bond of pure family love? Would we be loved and appreciated less than we are? Could any decent husband resist this kind of generous love or fail to thrive upon it?

This kind of self-deception can be expedient, even materially profitable for the time being. But the fact still remains: God cannot be deceived. He knows of our weakness long before we sob out that admission ourselves. He offers us the remedy through the voice of our confessor and we are too weak or too stubborn to accept it.

It seems easier somehow, to go on pretending that we do not know that we are cheating our own soul, our husband's soul, and the soul of our marriage of the graces needed to heal, strengthen, and draw us closer to God. Meanwhile the insidious evil spreads and burrows, undermining all that is good — all that is sacred in marriage. Can we wonder then what happens to sincerity, what happens to truth, and where these days is love?

We may deceive our husbands for a while. We can deceive ourselves so long as we convince ourselves that it is profitable for us to do so; all our lives if we so choose. But if such is our choice then we must face the reality that any profit realized during life will be canceled out at the moment of death, leaving only an eternal debt which never can be paid for we shall no longer have the ability to pay it. Our ability to pay will have been taken away from us.

God cannot be deceived.

There are all too many such women who insidiously and consistently undermine their own and their spouses' spiritual welfare because they simply will not face the truth about themselves. Searching their husbands' spiritual dispositions, their husbands' motives, their husbands' irresponsibility is the only soul-searching they do. They never search their own souls truthfully and sincerely because they cannot face the truth they would find there.

And they suffer. And many times they never resolve the resulting conflict until it is too late, and irreparable harm has been done.

Such a wife can never get the help she needs from a confessor, for she is not truthful with him. Even the co-operation of a well-disposed husband will not help her for she is living a lie.

The solution to such a wife's problem is found only within herself.

SCRUPULOSITY

We are sure we sidestep any traps set by the devil because nothing can induce us to miss our weekly confession. Our conscience is so "delicate" that we cannot bear even the thought of sin, and the remembrance of our past sins is a perpetual torment to us. Our confessions are thorough, so thorough in fact that they could be classed as general confessions. Our daily examinations of conscience are so exact that they are torturous involvements with all the sins we have ever committed from the moment we reached the age of reason to the present.

Our soul writhes from the shackling doubts holding it prisoner. We doubt our ability to make a good confession; we doubt our sincerity and true repentance; we doubt our confessor's divine power to absolve sin; we doubt God's assurance of mercy extended to sinners; we doubt that heaven was ever created for such as we. We are scrupulous and — because we are scrupulous — we excuse all these doubts away, then try to rest upon the mistaken conviction that scrupulosity and virtue are one and the same in God's sight.

So we keep digging around in our conscience and pulling out sins we may (or may not) have committed twenty-or-so years ago to see how they measure up and compare with out present-day sins. As we shake them out and dust them off, they look different than they did a decade ago, or last year, or last month, or even last week. We remember them. We scrutinize them. We reflect upon them and we confess them. Again.

Father tells us again what he has told us over and over: to let our past sins alone; to forget them; to place ourselves trustfully in God's hands. We would like to follow Father's advice, but we just cannot. Or if we do try to follow Father's advice we wind up feeling as though we have made a bad confession. We simply cannot trust ourselves.

So we keep remembering our past sins because we cannot trust ourselves. In reality it is not ourselves whom we distrust, but God. If we trusted God enough, and with childlike simplicity, we would never need to be concerned about trusting ourselves; we would *know* that we cannot trust ourselves and in that sure knowledge rest trustfully in God.

Or we keep remembering our sins because we are afraid we have not had sincere and proper sorrow for them. The saints, we are told, wept incessantly for their sins. We do not weep at all. All we seem capable of doing is remembering, and, in remembering, we forget that we can give God no better proof of our sorrow than the resolution to avoid sin now and in the future.

Then we may keep remembering our sins because we cannot ever be completely certain that our confessor's absolution has been effective for us. But then, can we ever hope to see the cleansing action of the priest's absolution? One moment we are scarlet; the next moment we are made as white as snow. Must we *see* or *feel* this transformation take place within the soul in order to believe? Suppose this vision were given to us, would our weakness be able to accept the evidence of it? Even in seeing we might doubt. It is better for us to kneel and in the darkness of secure faith repeat over and over: "I do believe, Lord: help my unbelief" (Mk. 9:23).

And finally, we may keep remembering our sins because we subconsciously enjoy the remembrance of them. This is a hard truth to accept, for the suppressed pleasure incited by reflection upon past sins adds a new sense of guilt. This in turn disturbs the soul with a strong current of remorse which may be mistaken for true contrition. It is also a hard truth to admit, for it is the same as admitting that the sins we have once committed in deed we keep on committing over and over again in thought. That this danger is real enough to cause fatal harm to the soul is emphasized by St. John of the Cross when he cautions aspirants to sanctity to leave past sins alone lest they become new occasions of sin upon reflection.

If our love for God, and our fear of God and the assurance our faith gives us as to God's mercy are not enough to calm our doubts, the realization of the danger hidden in scrupulosity should be enough to make us fly from reflection upon our past sins from this moment on.

Scrupulosity is dangerous and foolish. It is dangerous because its roots are in the kind of pride which takes a negative stand against certain tenets of faith. Such pride, if allowed to flourish unchecked, will finally plunge the soul into the dark cavern of despair where it can never hope to be pardoned.

Scrupulosity is foolish because we claim with one hand to be reaching for God, while with the other hand we remain attached to the sins which will keep us away from Him. Although we may think that we are turned toward God, in reality we are, in our scrupulosity, walking away from Him.

Scrupulosity is a delusive barrier to God's grace.

OVERSENSITIVENESS

Father So and So is our regular confessor. We go to great lengths to be sure to arrange our confession to coincide with the time we know he is in the confessional. Father So and So is so understanding and consoling when we speak to him of our spiritual difficulties. We just wouldn't think of going to confession to any other priest in the world — except when we happen to fall into an embarrassing sin. Then we go to even greater lengths to be sure Father So and So is not around to recognize the voice behind the sin. We may even chase all over town if we think our sin is serious enough, for we are very sensitive about such things.

Although there is nothing intrinsically wrong in seeking a confessor we do not know in order to be released from the burden of serious sin, the danger lies in our trying to cover up our being identified with sin. Some day, weighted down with serious sin, we may find ourselves kneeling before a priest who recognizes us. And because we just cannot bring ourselves to let Father know this awful truth about us, the harm is done. A bad confession is made and it may be months, years — or not at all — until the harm is rectified.

Or we are oversensitive about going to confession altogether. No matter which confessor we try, we never seem to be completely understood. They may understand our sins but they just do not seem to understand us. We could use a lot more sympathy from them and a lot less rebukes. After all, they should realize that we cannot always help the things we do; there are circumstances and people and a lot of other "et ceteras" with which we have to contend day in and day out. . . .

Whether or not our confessors know and recognize us or whether or not we think they understand us should make little difference if we go to confession primarily to avail ourselves of the sacramental grace. Of course there are times when we chafe under the discomfort of confession; but we should remember that although the sacrament of penance was instituted for our consolation in having a tangible assurance of God's pardon and mercy, it was not instituted for our comfort. We cannot very well be comfortable about our sins, for pride, which is the root of all our sins, is never comfortable when exposed.

Obviously the best cure for oversensitiveness would be to stop sinning altogether. But since even "the just man falls seven times a day," the next best cure is to establish a more obedient, docile, humble, and impersonal relationship with the confessor. Such a relationship will eventually cause the barrier of over-sensitiveness — which is nothing else than false pride — to give way to a more healthy perspective of true sanctity.

A UNIQUE RELATIONSHIP

God has given us confessors, but we are inclined to view our relationship with them through the foggy haze of our emotional involvement with confession. In other words we stay so pre-occupied with introspective discomfort caused by the shame and humiliation of our sins that we miss the whole point of that relationship. Our confessors are spiritual fathers who have a paternal concern for our spiritual welfare; yet we are inclined to consider them stern judges whom we approach only for reprimands and punishment.

The telling of our sins is only one aspect of confession just as listening to, and absolving our sins is just one part of Father's role as confessor. There is much more involved. If we can dis-associate ourselves from ourselves long enough to consider Father's role as confessor, the help he would give us, and something of what is expected of us, we would be taking an enormous step in the right direction.

Confession is very personal for us but it is very impersonal for the priest. Just because we are inclined to fall into a state of shock over a bit of scandal, especially if it concerns someone we know, does not prove that the priest has the same reaction to our sins. He is not only conditioned against such shock, he is likely to remain downright impassive no matter how enormous our sins may appear to us. He not only knows all about sin, he happens to be acquainted with more different kinds of sin than we would ever be clever enough to commit.

And knowing about sin he also understands our brushing with it, our falling into it, and our contamination from it. He also understands our groping misunderstanding of sin. And since he does understand us, our fallen human nature and our inherent shame and humiliation in having to admit our involvement with sin, we should never have the slightest misgivings about un-burdening our souls to any priest.

We should never be reluctant either in discussing, in the confessional, the intimate problems of our marriage. It is ridiculous to presume that the priest, because he is a celibate, can neither understand such things nor help us with them. The priest does not need to share the experience of our personal sins in order to help us on the way to spiritual recovery; yet many of us are guilty of this kind of foolish reasoning. It is just as ridiculous to presume that the only doctor who could cure us of pneumonia is the one who has died from it!

Rather than presume that priests' lack of experience in such things presupposes a lack of knowledge and understanding, we should try to realize that their very innocence and purity make their souls receptive to divinely infused understanding which far surpasses our own understanding, darkened as it is by sin and its effects.

Although our priests naturally conclude that we come to confession for the remission of sin, outside of the confessional they harbor no curiosity as to the state of our soul. Unless there is evidence to the contrary, they take it for granted that we are living in the state of grace. Nor do they use the confessional as a kind of peephole through which they might snatch a furtive glance at our souls in order to draw their own conclusions! These are the kind of vices we might claim, but God forbid that we use the distorted reflection of our own vices as a kind of lens in which we study the interior dispositions of our confessors. Their presence in the confessional is prompted by the sole duty of exercising their God-given power to cleanse us from sin and to offer the help we need to avoid sin in the future.

Instead of being overembarrassed by what we have to tell the priest in confession, it would be more helpful if we concentrated instead upon what the priest does for us. The spiritual transaction which takes place in the confessional between the priest and ourselves can be likened to an exchange. We hand over to him the tattered and contaminated garment of our sins and in exchange he places upon our soul the shining garment of sanctifying grace.

And we can thank God over and over that this spiritual transaction is not a mere superficiality. So deep and so miraculous is the reality of what confession does for us, that face to face with it we must be lost in wonder and amazement. The sin which has been a torment of shame and confusion is gone, and the priest, who may remember the sin but only to help us make reparation for it, forgets at once the sinner. His faith is such that under his absolving hand he knows the sin has been removed and is gone and so cannot ever be identified with us unless we will to make it part of us again.

Once we have an appreciation and understanding of the impersonal and objective relationship of the confessor toward the penitent we should carry our part of the relationship one step farther. We should choose, and stay with, a regular confessor. And we should make ourselves known to him. This does not necessarily mean that we need tell him our name, address, phone number, etc., rather we should establish with him a continuity between our confessions so that he may more easily discern the path our spirituality is taking according to how we have, or have not, followed his advice.

For example we might say to him: "Father, last week you advised such and such a practice, or mortification, or renunciation . . ." and then go on to explain how we tried successfully, or otherwise, to carry out his advice. Let us never be inhibited, though, in stating the weaknesses which so often cancel out our good intentions. It is our intentions in which Father is most interested. If they are good then the sacramental grace of confession along with Father's help will take care of the weaknesses in due course.

God has given us confessors. Let us appreciate them, for their worth to us is inestimable. There is no more consoling nor spiritually profitable relationship on earth than the one between the sincere penitent and his spiritual director, impersonal though it may seem.

Renewed and strengthened by the sacramental grace received regularly in frequent confessions, our soul is disposed to take on a new spiritual vigor. Meanwhile, under the confessor's watchful guidance we gradually acquire a self-knowledge which is altogether different from any knowledge we have ever had of ourselves. Stripped gradually of our pretenses, our deceptions, and our opinions, we come to recognize ourselves a little more clearly in the light of God's reflection; a light usually dispensed in the darkness of the confessional.

UTILIZING THE TIME

Saturday nights are busy nights for all Catholic priests. Heavy doors swing silently open and shut as Catholics from all neighborhoods and all classes of society "go to confession." While we kneel, either during our examination of conscience or while we are saying our penance, we are aware of the constant stream of penitents coming into church, standing in line, entering the confessional, and leaving. It is always the same. Whether we come early or late, hoping to find a break in the lines, there is seldom one.

Many times these long lines are a source of annoyance to us. Confession takes more time than we had planned to give; for getting it over with as quickly and as painlessly as possible is all too often our only concern. And the half hour that could have been used to advantage while patiently waiting is thrown away as useless. This half hour could have been fruitful. We could have used it profitably in meditation, in thanksgiving, and in reparation.

Our meditation could have taken the path that leads to exploring more thoughtfully the Mystical Body of Christ and our relationship with all other members of this Body; especially those sharing the same privilege as ours this night — all those going to confession. We could have prayed for them asking God to give them, and us, the grace to receive this sacrament worthily and fruitfully. Our prayers could have gone out to those who should be going to confession but who are not because of negligence or hardheartedness. We could have begged God to bring them back to the sacraments again.

And we could have spent some time in thoughtfully thanking God for what He had given us this night: the desire to draw closer to Him through the confessional, and for our confessors who remain in the confessional until the last penitent is absolved.

In humble gratitude we could have reflected upon the important task our confessors perform for us in helping us atone for the sins we have committed. For when the priest leaves the confessional, no matter how long and tiring the ordeal has been, his work is only partly done. He will now take upon himself a new burden of reparation in order to help fill up what is lacking in us. Another Christ carrying another cross; being crucified again for the sins we have committed that the life-giving Blood of Christ may keep flowing endlessly through His Mystical Body — ever renewing, regenerating, and ever giving more vigorous life to us the weaker members.

The time that was ours to give during these moments of waiting, we could have offered as little grains of incense that, set burning with God's love, would have helped us atone for our own sins and for the sins of others.

The sacrament of penance should be a joy and a consolation for all of us, for as we voluntarily open the door of the confessional and kneel before our confessor we admit ourselves into the anteroom to sanctity. In the darkness of this small room our soul becomes again the bright mirror reflecting God's image. As we leave the confessional we have within our own hands the ability to deface this image again or to keep it shining and beautiful and to go eventually through this looking glass, which is ourselves, into the Garden Enclosed — God Himself.

REFLECTIONS ON SIN

To know Jesus Crucified is to know God's horror of sin; its guilt could be washed away only in the Precious Blood of God's only begotten Son become Man.

Perhaps the greatest sin in the world today is that men have begun to lose the sense of sin. Smother that, deaden it — it can hardly be wholly cut out from the heart of man — let it not be awakened by any glimpse of the God Man dying on Golgotha's cross to pay the penalty of sin, and what is there to hold back the hordes of God's enemy from over-running the selfishness, the pride, the sensuality and unlawful ambitions of sinful man? (Pius XII, October 26, 1946.)

CONTRADICTION OF SIN

Holiness and sinfulness have about the same kind of compelling attraction for us, yet when it comes to embracing either of them wholeheartedly, our courage fails. Not many of us would have the courage to be the sinner Mary Magdalen was, nor the great saint she is. We are content rather to nibble alternately at the apple of temptation and the bread of sanctity.

Sin is just as attractive to us as it was to Eve; yet remembering Eve, we are afraid to take a good-size bite. We forget, though, that in nibbling at forbidden fruit we are in danger of having the devil shove it down our throats, leaving us choking and wondering how it happened. Holiness, too, is as attractive to

us as it is to any of the saints, yet when we sample this unleavened bread we find it too dry and tasteless for our self-
satisfying appetite; and turning away from it we forego the only
food upon which our soul can thrive.

We protest that we have no intention of offending God;
that we want no traffic with the devil. We want only to be
good wives and mothers and because this is our desire, we
consider ourselves already paragons of virtue. We take infinite
pains to clothe our faults, failings, and sins with virtuous excuses. We develop quite a nimble facility for skirting the positive
evils which would cause raised eyebrows among our friends and
neighbors, confining our indulgence to only the respectable sins
— sins everyone else commits without being criticized or condemned. Joining the parade of other good wives and mothers
we are content to remain lost in that comfortable mediocrity.

And yet our lives are spent seeking the Good! More often than
we care to remember though, we have found that the good
for which we reached was nothing more than the dry pod of
sin which, when grasped, scattered its bitter seeds of evil upon
us and those around us. All our lives we hunger and thirst for
Good. Over and over we find that we settle for less than the
Good for which we hoped; and in the compromise, possess only
dissatisfaction and frustration instead of the peace and joy the
perfect Good would have given us.

We do not want to sin and yet we must always have to admit
in truth that we are sinners!

As mature Catholic women, we are inclined to rest upon the
conviction that we know all we should know about sin. Mortal
sin is a grievous offense against the law of God; venial sin is a
slight offense against the law of God. Since we chanted this fundamental definition of sin from our first catechism, our knowledge
of sin has been supplemented by our reading about it, our being
warned about it, our hearing sermons and instructions concerning it, and our firsthand experience with it. We are certain we

know a lot about sin. Actually we know very little about it, and the understanding we have of sin is even less than our knowledge of it.

We know sin is an offense against God; we know that it is evil; we know it can be the cause of our eternal damnation. Sin is all of these things, yet to us as sinners sin apparently is none of these things. If it were in anticipation and in actuality we never would sin, for no one nor anything could induce us to sin. We come closer to our own understanding and knowledge of sin when we admit that to us, sin is nothing more than forbidden pleasure. We desire, more or less inordinately, the pleasure of sin while at the same time we hope that by some direct intervention from God we can avoid contamination from it. We want the good and we pluck the evil.

THEOLOGY OF SIN

Theologians explain this confusing disorder as the wound left in our soul from original sin; the wound which contains a predisposition to the infection of sin. Since we have been made to the image and likeness of God, our soul can never rest nor find fruition outside of Him. He is the Good we forever seek and if we do not seek this Good in God Himself, we are constantly seeking good in a substitute for Him: in ourselves, in other creatures, in material things, and in sin itself.

Our will reaches out constantly to embrace that which is lovable, yet it loves only what it sees and knows and possesses. Our will sees, knows, and embraces or rejects only what is presented to it as lovable or detestable by our intellect. If our intellect had never been darkened by original sin and blinded further by our own personal sins and their effects, this faculty of the soul would be enlightened to the extent in which it would know God as the perfect Truth; our will would embrace God and love Him as the perfect Good and heaven would be more easily attained; for this knowledge and love of God is heaven begun for us on earth.

This may be a simple theological explanation of sin, but we know that the personal problem of sin is far from simple. We just cannot ever seem to be able to keep our sense of eternal values in order. Like a child at a carnival we reach into a grab bag and pick out the gaudiest package we can find, hoping that what is inside is even more exciting. Upon opening it we find that we have only the crumpled wrapping and an empty box. We have nothing and we keep nothing, and, in trying again, we pass up the gifts in the plain or unattractive wrappings for they do not appeal to us. We are not even interested as to what may be inside, but prefer to keep choosing what is bright and attractive at first glance.

And this is why we sin. Our intellect, using its power to reason, to rationalize, and to discern finds good wherever it searches, whether the good is real — as only it can be in God or only apparent as it is in sin. The intellect presents this good to the will, and the will in accepting it chooses deliberately the Good which is God, or deliberately rejects God in choosing a creature, a pleasure, or an ambition which has been substituted for Him.

Once we have had the misfortune of choosing the apparent good which is sin, we are bound then to choose between two paths going in opposite directions: one leading back to God by way of the confessional, or one leading farther away from Him by way of habitual sin. One serious fall may be all we need to teach us something of what sin does to the soul. The remembrance of the remorse and suffering this estrangement caused will be enough, with God's grace, to keep us from serious sin in the future.

And one serious fall may be all we need to start us dashing headlong into hell, for we may remember only the pleasure, only the exciting sense of illicit freedom of sinning which, while remaining so attractive, blankets any remorse or sorrow we may feel. We are in danger, then, of going from one sin to another;

spending our lives and ourselves in feeding the fire of temptation — the fire which must eventually destroy us.

If we were not so blind in our sins and if we were not so comfortable in our blindness, we might try to shake off the darkness which obscures the light of divine Truth, so that our will might cleave more strongly to the Good which is God. But like the blind we are afraid to suffer the discomfort which may result in more suffering because our eyes cannot stand the light, accustomed as they are to darkness.

We are afraid that if our relationship with God becomes too intimate we shall have to relinquish all our pet sins. Our small and harmless indulgences will be taken away from us and we shall be left with nothing but God. The thought frightens us. It is too awesome; too terrifying. We could never spend every moment with God. We could never be at ease! We feel much more secure acting like ostriches and hoping that because we do not see God, He does not see us.

Since sin leaves no visible marks of contamination, and since no one sees them, or our soul, we may reason that our own personal sins are our own personal affair. We may carry this foolish reasoning further and try to convince ourselves that God Himself does not see them; or if He does He ignores them; or if He does not ignore them, by the time we come to die we will have thought up enough clever arguments to excuse them away. God could not possibly deprive us of heaven. We are much too good for hell!

All of this when our faith assures us that God is a most benevolent and loving father; that His beloved Son was crucified for the very sins we would cherish; that in spite of our sinfulness He is ever ready to forgive us and set our heart burning with the flame of His own divine love. All of this and we prefer to remain stifled in the darkness of our hidden sins; not knowing and caring less what these cherished sins are doing to our soul.

MORTAL SIN

We should never forget that mortal sin is serious sin and all mortal sin is serious. Crime in general we are inclined to regard as shockingly serious sin, yet sins of expedience, ambition, or convenience we are inclined to regard as not really serious, even though they may be classed as mortal sins. One mortal sin of expedience can merit hell for us just as surely as would pre-meditated murder — even though we may shudder at the comparison!

Sins of expedience, convenience, or ambition may slip very easily into our lives for they have become the socially acceptable sins. They are the sins we "use" to realize an advantage which virtue might not, or would not provide. Two of the most common of these sins are invalid marriage and birth prevention.

Using any of these socially acceptable sins for material gain or for any other reason is the same as robbing our soul of its rightful inheritance. We may not have the courage to rob a bank to get the money we think we need, but it does not take much courage to slide into the habit of robbing our spiritual safe deposit box and spending the treasure we should be laying up for eternity.

So we use the sins which do not seem so serious in exchange for such things as a higher standard of living, the further pamper-ing of our already pampered children, social prestige, "necessary" luxuries, expensive clothes and cosmetics to keep us beautiful — and cover up the insidious cancer eating at our soul. For all these things we pilfer the payment from eternity that we might enjoy our temporal life more thoroughly (we think), and we push the thought of heaven and God into some distant cubby-hole, saving it for some future time when these expensive commodities no longer make so many demands upon us. We neither consider nor worry about the fact that persistence in the state into which these sins plunge the soul cancels out any eternal reward we may think we may claim from the other virtues which we practice with such careful nicety.

If we deliberately choose the temporal reward rather than the eternal that is what we shall have, for mortal sin cannot be rewarded either on earth or in heaven — no matter what our convictions may be to the contrary. Only virtue may realize a twofold reward, if God sees fit to render it. The virtuous may prosper in life and yet go on to enjoy eternal life also. The sinner in justice may not.

We may think we are clever in using mortal sin for an advantage, but even in this life mortal sin gives the sinner no real reward. We may become wealthy or socially prominent, but we shall also become miserable. In the state of mortal sin the soul can find no peace.

Mortal sin enmeshes our soul in a web of confusion and in this confusion all our faculties and emotions are thrown into restless disorder. In this state hatred thrives. Our relationship with God and with humanity becomes darkened with this vice. The emotion which we would tag with the name of love is no longer love in the true sense because our love, no longer pure, is divorced from its true source, divine love.

If we think that we can remain in mortal sin and yet go on loving purely, unselfishly, and enduringly, we are deceiving ourselves. All we need do to verify this truth is to scan our daily newspaper for the evidence that conjugal, and even maternal, love rooted in mortal sin ends in murder, suicide, insanity, divorce, child abandonment. We may argue that none of these things are likely to happen to us! We are good wives and mothers! We may avoid some of these tragic ends, or all of them, but unless our love is rooted in virtue and in God we shall avoid heaven also.

Love in the soul of those in mortal sin is nothing more than a perverted caricature of what should be sublime and holy. If we persist in mortal sin we come to love only those persons, or things which add fuel to the incinerator of our self-love where smolder all the vices which we decry in others and which we blindly nourish in ourselves. We love only that which inflates our pride, stimulates our lust, gorges our greed, and pampers our sloth. Even this poor excuse for love must ultimately degenerate into hatred; a hatred which accuses all of these things as our destroyers and finally at hatred turned inward upon ourselves because we have eaten these vile fruits.

No sinner loves mortal sin any more than a drug addict loves heroin. What is loved is the pleasure, the release from conventional morality, and the false sense of freedom this release temporarily gives. Then we hate the moral hang-over — the person, place, or thing responsible for our misery, and finally ourselves for having been so blinded by what is now nothing but dust and ashes of remorse and despair. To cure this spiritual hangover, we seek forgetfulness again in the pleasure of sin all the while rejecting the obvious cure of repentance and atonement as too painful and too humiliating.

Only one mortal sin defaces the image of God in the soul. Could we understand, then, what habitual mortal sin must do; except to consider that we who have been made to the image and likeness of God have become the image and likeness of Satan: the father of lies, the source of all darkness, the malicious vacuum of hatred.

Could we ever hope for heaven in this disordered state? Or could God in justice invite such a soul to inhabit heaven where all souls rest in the perfect order of divine love? Or could God in justice pardon us after death if we despised any help He offered us during life, too proud to seek it or accept it?

If our sentiments are such that they exclude God during life they will not change with death. At the time of death we shall keep our sentiments; only our point of view will be changed. In the light of divine truth we shall be overwhelmed with our tremendous folly and we shall see all things, even sin, in their proper order. We shall see ourselves, and in seeing ourselves we shall know that heaven cannot be for us and we shall try to fly from heaven and from God as we should have flown from the world and from sin. We shall find that we are just where we wanted to be during life, and where we must be now: in hell. And there we may give vent to all the unbridled malice, passion, and rage of which we are capable; in misery and without satisfaction and rest, for hell is confusion, disorder, and despair. No one will expect us to practice self-control in hell — nor could we if we so desired.

VENIAL SIN

If we have a healthy repugnance for mortal sin and avoid it all our lives, or at least get rid of it in the confessional as soon as possible after commission, we should become saints. Unfortunately we do not. In spite of the fact that we are careful to avoid serious sin and pride ourselves further in the fact that we spend our lives basking in the warmth of sanctifying grace, we never seem to acquire any more than an anemic, apathetic spirituality. Without the restrictions and degenerating effects of mortal sin our soul should turn naturally to God, to be filled by Him with all the necessary graces and helps to make them vigorous and strong in His love, and to make them fruitful gardens filled with flowering virtues.

Our spirituality always seems to fall short, not only of the goal of perfection we would like to set for ourselves but also, we are afraid, of the goal we suspect that God has set for us. We are satisfied because our gardens are green. We enjoy "basking" so much that we forget that our spiritual garden needs more than an occasional clipping to keep it productive. We let the weeds grow; the weeds which are our venial sins, our attachments to all that is not God, our petty bad habits which we enjoy because we are convinced that they are harmless.

A garden full of weeds would never win a prize! Yet as spiritual gardeners most of us never go beyond keeping the weeds trimmed. We like our gardens just the way they are. Expecting God to water them with the dew of His consolation and to warm them with the sunshine of His love, we neglect the digging and the cultivating. This work entrusted to us, seems too hard and too bothersome.

And the weeds prosper, for no matter how carefully we trim them, their roots are strong and their growth vigorous. Spreading beneath the surface, their roots sap the strength of the virtues trying to grow and bloom. Their stems thicken and send out fibrous stalks and choking tendrils until what was once a promising garden becomes an unproductive plot of ground.

A soul, planned and planted by the divine Gardener to be a garden enclosed where the Trinity would love to dwell, becomes nothing more than an empty enclosure. To such souls our Lord was speaking when He said: "I would thou wert cold, or hot. But because thou art lukewarm . . . I will begin to vomit thee out of my mouth" (Apoc. 3:16).

Venial sin is not serious sin, and a million venial sins could not make one mortal sin, nor cause us to be lost forever. We are not even obligated to confess them and so we are inclined to ignore them. Venial sin is not serious in itself, but we keep our soul wide open for trouble by the habitual commission of any of them.

Venial sins such as little lies told for convenience or to exaggerate our own importance or the importance of those we cherish; lies told to cover up our failings or our mistakes; little white lies harmless perhaps in themselves. We cling to them; our little lies grow strong in the pernicious tendency to darken divine truth in our soul. And what happens! The soul is prepared for the stealthy entrance of the father of lies who may trap us in the biggest lie of all: a mortal sin, which as temptation did not look serious at all.

Uncharitable thoughts. Nasty little opinions which we refrain from speaking at first because they are below the standard of what is expected of our charity. Allowed to stay in our mind, encouraged and reflected upon, we find that we can no longer savor such thoughts in silence and they become sins of slander and detraction. Uncharitable thoughts, uncharitable words, uncharitable actions — or at least the neglect of charitable deeds! We become uncharitable and say we love God. Yet God is charity and with our venial sins against charity we smother the growth of His divine charity within us and wonder if prejudice and envy and hatred creep in.

Impurity. Little impurities which grow and spread and keep us from being numbered among the children who are pure of heart, and whom God loves so dearly as His own. Not only the impurity which connotes a lack of chastity, but also clouds all our relationships with others whom we should be loving and serving purely in Christ, but whom we love and serve for our own advantage. Impurity dims the luster of all the virtues and obscures the Sun of Purity so necessary for our soul's eternal welfare, until the fog becomes so thick that we are in danger of losing the sight and the warmth of this Sun forever.

Venial sin is not serious sin, but it is serious enough to prevent us from growing up in Christ; if it does not weaken our spiritual reserves enough to allow us to fall a step lower — into mortal sin.

COMPANIONATE SIN

As wives and mothers we have a unique problem concerning sin. Although the very intimacies of the married state should be wholly conducive to the mutual sanctification of husband and wife, these same intimacies can be equally conducive to sinning.

The most fertile area in which these seeds of contradiction can thrive is in the conjugal relationship. Among the married more sins have been committed under the false guise of love than for any other reason. When temptation arises, a loving companion would seem almost a kind of insurance against personal involvement. The idea of togetherness and mutual sharing seem somehow to diminish the evil and seriousness of sin.

Once a "mutual sin" is committed, though, there is no consolation at all in what seemed like a mutual sharing of guilt. The common failing of the married to share their sins does not result in a common sharing of guilt. Although our sins may seem mutual, our guilt must always remain personal. We may walk into sin with a companion, but we must walk into the confessional alone.

It is in this area of conjugal relationship too that spiritual incompatibility is most often a serious problem. This is especially true if one of the married partners considers such transgressions as part of the marriage right, while the other party has a more delicate conscience concerning such sins.

Spiritual incompatibility here will cause conflict, with the more conscientious partner being the most tormented victim; the conflict will inevitably result in one of two things: a break with sin or a break with confession. Not even a confessor can resolve such a conflict for one married partner if the other rejects the sacramental graces which would help eliminate such sins from a marriage.

Here personal responsibility will help take up the slack which spiritual incompatibility causes. The conscientious partner must put on virtue to a heroic degree in order to prevent the devil from destroying all that is holy in marriage. But such virtue must be true, strong, and sincere.

Before we give in so easily to the mutual "enjoyment" of sinning for whatever reason, we should seriously consider our personal responsibility in this matter. It is easier to fight a temptation before it leads to habitual sin than it is to try to resolve a conflict which might arise from trying to make a break with sin. This is especially true if one partner may like the pleasure of sin more than the hardship virtue may impose. Every sin shared with a spouse causes the spiritual welfare of each individual to be undermined. Personal sanctification is endangered along with the sanctification of the spouse.

In the day to day living out of the marriage vocation there

are many opportunities to give good example by the practice of virtue and there are many opportunities to be an occasion of sin through bad example. Many of our own personal sins, and many of the sins committed around us could be avoided if we took a positive stand for virtue.

Think how many sins of anger and rash judgment would be avoided if we would only cultivate the virtue of patience. How many family quarrels start because of the common failing of picking up a misconstrued comment and batting it around until it explodes into bitterness and hatred. The painful bruises, the festering wounds are not always physical, but they are none the less painful, and even more serious since they are spiritual.

As the saying goes, it takes two to start an argument. Many an argument would never start if we learned to keep our mouths shut — or better yet if we learned to change the subject with good humor and patience. Once quarreling and anger have inflicted their pain upon two who are supposed to love each other, there is little consolation in where the blame lies. In such a case our personal responsibility of avoiding the sin of anger lies shattered at our feet, and all we have is the questionable consolation of knowing that, besides offending God, we have injured the one we are supposed to love and we have undermined the spiritual welfare of those around us by bad example.

How many times, too, by indifference to our own personal responsibility concerning sin, do we actually plant the seeds of evil in our children's souls.

How many children reach adolescence with contempt for authority because their parents have actually fostered this contempt by openly criticizing all those placed in the position of authority — whether they be priests, nuns, teachers or law-enforcement officers. Such children never learn to overlook human weakness and failings in individuals vested with authority. They never learn that authority itself comes from God and such authority relegates peace all the way down the line even to the least subject, so long as this authority is respected and accepted with obedience and docility. Instead, such children prepare to take their places in the world with the conviction that authority is synonymous with corruption and are in danger of spending all their lives trying to prove that this is true.

Unless a child learns respect for parental authority first — and at an early age — he is not likely to acquire this virtue later, and on his own. It is our personal responsibility to teach our children reverence and respect for those placed over them. We also have a personal responsibility to act always in a manner worthy of their respect.

How many young people cheat their way through school, then face the world with the shifty-eyed suspicion that everyone is out to cheat them. Husbands and wives who lie to each other and to their children cannot expect their children to mature as honest, truthful individuals. Children are not so easily deceived. It does not take a child long to learn to resort to lies for the same reasons his parents do — to escape responsibility, to avoid punishment, or to gain some otherwise unattainable end. Unless the light of truth lights up our own personal virtue we are not likely to have children who appreciate truthfulness and honesty.

How many children are deprived of the happy carefree joy of living as beloved children of God because they have never been instructed in the goodness of their heavenly Father; who never learn the soul-satisfying serenity of trustful prayer because they have never been taught to pray; who never hear God's name spoken except in blasphemy!

But, you may say, you are talking about delinquents. These are not our children!

Aren't they?

If these are not our children, and if they are not the victims of our own irresponsibility and involvement with sin — with or without the corroboration of a spouse — then there would be no delinquents among our children. There would be no broken marriages among us.

GOD'S SENSE OF SIN

Our sins are personal only in the sense that we personally commit them and are personally responsible for them. Once a sin is committed we can no longer claim it as a purely personal thing, for its effects go out from us in many directions. First, sin undermines the spiritual health and vigor of our own soul; it undermines the spiritual well-being of our spouse, and our children; it undermines the sanctity of our marriage; then spreads even further to lessen the vitality of the whole Mystical Body of Christ. Sin is, then, something else besides a personal indulgence. It is a diabolical instrument in our hand used with malicious intent upon the Body of Christ.

If only we would ponder the realization of this truth. If only we would take the time to meditate upon this fact we would come to understand something of God's viewpoint concerning sin. We prefer instead to consider our own personal sins as our own personal indulgences and confine our horror over sin to the sins committed by others.

Looking back to the time of Christ's Passion, we are inclined to feel a little relieved that we were not there; that we were not among the ones responsible for His brutal Passion and death. We would hate to think the responsibility ours.

Yet it is ours, for we were there! Every individual born before or after Christ's time was there, for we were all present to Him in our sinfulness. We were as present to Him then as we are present to Him now; for in the mind of God every individual has been present to Him for all eternity. Our birth, life, and death seem only an accidental circumstance to us; but to God, our birth, life, and death is an eternal reality.

Because our own personal sins happen to be our pleasure two thousand years after Christ's agony, does not mean that they have no bearing upon His Passion. Our sins were heaped upon that crushing burden which pressed the very blood from every pore in His body. Our sins of pride plaited that thorny crown and pressed it into His head. The scourge which ripped the flesh from His body was wielded with the fury of our sensuality. The nails, the cross, the spear — all the instruments of the Passion were fashioned from our sins for one purpose: to be rid of Christ. But the very instruments we would use to destroy Him, He takes from us and with His unfathomable love turns them into the instruments of our redemption.

Can we still remain complacent in our sins, just because the Passion of Christ took place so long ago? If we can, we are living in blind delusion. The Passion of Christ did not end with His burial. It still goes on in His Mystical Body, and will continue to go on until the end of time.

So we keep on sinning and the Mystical Body of Christ goes on suffering; writhing in agony, yet praying with Christ: "Father, forgive them for they know not what they do" — praying for us while suffering from the effects of our own personal sins.

St. Paul tells us: ". . . what is lacking of the sufferings of Christ I fill up in my flesh for his body, which is the Church . . ." (Col. 1:24). Incorporated into this Body at baptism, we also are supposed to make up what is wanting in the Passion of Christ. Not that anything is wanting so far as Christ is concerned; what is wanting is our co-operation — our own personal participation in His redemptive sacrifice.

And we keep on sinning. We take the love He would offer us and throw it back at Him. We take the graces He won for us at such an awful price, and with our sins, fashion them again into the instruments which would crucify Him and put to death the life He has given us.

Our own personal sins may not seem so horrible to us, but to God, the horror of sin is Christ Crucified.

WATCH AND PRAY

Many times during every day that we live it is necessary that we exercise our God-given faculties of intelligence, discernment, and down-to-earth common sense in keeping our homes and family relations in order. It is a source of wonder that we ignore using these same faculties to keep our spirituality in order and to keep sin where it belongs — out of our life.

What we need to do to avoid sin — all sin, mortal and venial — is to be as intelligent and as sensible about sin as we are about any other danger which may threaten our lives, our homes, and our families. With a spiritual backbone strengthened with God's grace, all we need further to do is to take the necessary precautions against sin as we would against any hazard. Any other method employed to avoid sin is useless, otherwise we may be approaching sin instead of avoiding it as we thought.

For example, it is a waste of time to cultivate a kind of hair trigger, shock reaction to sin. To think that because we are shocked by sin, especially the sins of others, that we shall avoid it, is a fatal mistake; for what shocks us today in others may seem, tomorrow, to be perfectly justifiable in ourselves.

It is also a waste of spiritual energy to cultivate an inordinate fear of the devil, and by resting upon the conviction that by being afraid of him we shall avoid sin. Just as soon as Satan discovers that we are afraid of him, he may come to us disguised as our bosom friend and we will welcome him with open arms.

Besides being objective and truthful about sin, especially about our own personal involvement with sin, we should never forget that prayer which brings us God's help is the only sure precaution upon which we may depend. Our prayer should be a sincere petition that we be preserved from sin, as the Psalmist prayed: "O Lord, set a watch before my mouth, a guard at the door of my lips. Let not my heart incline to the evil of engaging in deeds of wickedness" (Ps. 140:3–4). Prayer is the most powerful shield against sin.

Starting with ourselves, then, and fortified with God's grace and strengthened with prayer and the sacraments, we should begin by giving sin no place in our lives and in our homes. This is our first field of endeavor; the small mission which we control and from which goodness may radiate to the far-flung corners of the world.

This is how we start bringing souls to God. Despite the materialistic atmosphere which surrounds us, we have the power to start the pilgrimage which will bring more and more of God's children back to Him. God's children are also our children, to hide from Him or to lead to Him as we choose. And we need not be afraid that bringing souls to God is a job too big for us, it is not. For this we entered God's plan which made us wives and mothers — our vocation.

If we are careful to keep our lives and our homes as gardens of virtue, then our sons and daughters in maturing and leaving us will carry the seeds we have given them to be planted in other places. And we need not worry, for our children will know how to plant them, to care for them and to bring them to fruition. They will have learned these lessons from us.

This is the sacred trust which has been given to us as Catholic wives and mothers: that we become saints and that we people heaven with saints. This is God's will for us, and so it can be done. Not so easily perhaps, but it can be done!

This work can be done by those of us who have been sinful, but who would follow now the path blazed by Mary Magdalen. She exchanged the rash temerity which had plunged her into sin for the supreme courage to love God fearlessly and in doing so became a greater saint that she was a sinner. God's will can also be done by those of us who have never lost God's love and friendship through mortal sin, but who may feel that a high degree of sanctity is only for the courageous. Actually it is. But if we fear hell, we need never fear God, except with a holy fear which will bring us closer to Him and draw from Him the courage we need to aspire, as did Therese of the Child Jesus, to heroic holiness.

SEEKING AND FINDING GOD

To seek out God, to find Him, it is enough to enter into your-
selves, morning, night, or at any moment of the day. If you are
joyfully in the state of grace, you will see in the intimacy of your
soul with the eyes of faith God ever present as an immensely
kind Father, ready to hear your requests and tell you also what
He expects of you . . . (Pius XII, February 2, 1941).

SEEKING AND FINDING GOD IN CONFLICT

CONFLICT HAS A PURPOSE

The way to God is obscure for everyone. Just because we are
married does not mean that the temptations and conflicts which
are peculiarly ours are diametrically opposed to perfection. Before
we fall into the fallacy of believing that marriage contradicts our
whole conception of holiness, we should remember that the contradiction does not lie within our marriage, but within ourselves.

We are all born into contradiction, and the flesh will war
against the spirit until we draw our last breath. What we need
to realize is that every time this warfare takes place within us,
God is also working within us; purifying, refining, preparing us
for a closer union with Him. We should never forget that the
most dangerous temptations are not necessarily the searing temptations of the flesh. We need especially to be on guard against

the subtle ones — temptations aimed at the very heart of our vocation; conflicts which have their beginning in boredom, restlessness, frustrations, wishful thinking.

Our conflicts can have one of two effects. We can follow temptation's lead and use conflict as an excuse to escape; or we can stand firm in our conflicts and allow God to draw us to Himself.

If we generously accept God as He gives Himself to us in conflict, He will teach us that the human heart, rendered empty and desolate by suffering, is the only cup worthy to hold the Living Water — Christ Himself.

We are not likely to become canonized saints from the endurance of one interior conflict, any more than we are likely to become perfect mothers from the endurance of one pregnancy. Just as conception is merely the beginning of motherhood, so is the seed of grace hidden in interior conflict the beginning of sanctity.

In conception the seed, having all the potentialities of a new human being, must be brought forth, protected, nourished; now the cause of sorrow, another time the cause of joy. So it is with that particular seed of sanctity which has its beginnings in conflict. This seed, planted by God Himself, has all the potentialities of the new man which must be brought forth in us and cherished with like solicitude that Christ might be perfected in us.

In speaking of the tribulations which are the ultimate cause of our sanctification, St. Paul says:

"For this reason I bend my knees to the Father of our Lord Jesus Christ, from whom all fatherhood in heaven and on earth receives its name, that he may grant you from his glorious riches to be strengthened with power through his Spirit unto the progress of the inner man; and to have Christ dwelling through faith in your hearts: so that, being rooted and grounded in love, you may be able to comprehend with all the saints what is the breadth and the length and the height and depth, and to know

Christ's love which surpasses knowledge, in order that you may be filled unto all the fullness of God" (Eph. 3:14–19).

No vessel can be filled unless it is first empty, and the human heart is no exception; filled as it is with self, with sin, with inordinate attachments. God's pure love in such an environment would be smothered before it had a chance to germinate.

And so, when the soul begins sincerely seeking Him, He begins "emptying it out" by way of interior conflict that it may begin to be filled with the fullness of Christ.

For in this "emptiness" God is found — in the center of the soul. This is the quiet retreat for which the soul yearns. But do not ever forget that the entrance into this domain can be gained only in the patient and loving endurance of the daily sufferings which God wills to send.

SEEKING AND FINDING GOD IN PRAYER

PRACTICE OR DISPOSITION

Hidden in conflict, God moves the soul to seek Him in prayer. He does this, not merely to emphasize our helpless dependence upon Him (although we learn that too), but because He would reveal Himself now as a Friend. A severe interior conflict successfully combated may leave us feeling weak and shaken, but it also leaves us with an inherent knowledge that *Someone* has pulled us through. We turn naturally to God in relief and thanksgiving.

We find, to our surprise, that we *want to pray!*

It is such a delightful surprise to find that prayer has taken on a whole new concept! The discovery that prayer seems no longer a boring obligation, more easily forgotten than practiced, immediately sparks an inclination to make an endless mental list of all the prayerful exercises to be carried out from now on, because we want to explore prayer from every possible angle and we want to plunge into it and lose ourselves in it and if we

can stop long enough to catch a breath — here — precisely is
where we need to apply the check reins!

New resolutions are good. God expects them from us. The
desire to be lost in prayer is good. God wants us to want to
lose ourselves in Him. What we have to watch is the enthusiasm.
Carried away by too much enthusiasm there is always the danger
that we may wind up lost, but not in God. And being just plain
lost can be a tragic end to a good beginning!

So how do we proceed? Since circumstances for a wife and
mother are more general than particular, the safest way, probably, is to pursue a general plan for prayer. Particulars may
always be picked up and worked in later by the individual. So
for the purpose at hand we shall stick to generalities.

The first and most important thing to remember — inclinations notwithstanding — is that we are not abandoning our way
of life for the life of prayer! A whole month's meditation upon
this fact alone would not be too much time to spend on this
thought!

And here is why:

If, despite yourself, you feel that you are being drawn away
from the world, do not worry about it, you are. But not in
the same sense that one is being drawn away from the world in
order to enter the religious life. Walking out of the front door
and into the convent is not the only way to leave the world!

What is experienced at this time is the "pull" which would
loosen us from the attractions, distractions, and pleasures with
which the world entices us. It is not ever to be considered as
an attraction which would pull us away from the place in which
God has put us. The place in which God has put us is *here*,
in the home, and that is precisely where He wants us to stay.
And so the first thing we must realize is that, although the
soul may "feel" drawn to God, we — ourselves — are not going
anywhere.

The second thing to remember is our *way of life* as wife and
mother. Just because we feel an attraction for prayer, does not

mean that we are supposed to turn ourselves into Mother Superior! A strict spiritual schedule may be fine for a convent, but it can be fatal for a home!

God does not expect us to begin by herding the family together for long recitations which, for them, could be tiresome and boring. He wants us to start first with ourselves, that learning to know Him more intimately in prayer, the fruits of our personal prayer may overflow into the rest of the family.

Of course, there is always the possibility that a stepped-up prayer schedule is just what your family has been waiting for; but if yours is a normal family, they will be more inclined to rebel than to accede. Suggest it if you will, but do not force the issue. If members of the family have been praying privately all this time, respect their privacy and they will respect yours. We cannot start *dragging* a family to God, we may only *lead* them.

This is why so many of our good intentions fail. In our new found enthusiasm, we start out trying to organize and convert everyone else, then fall away ourselves, because no one — *simply no one* — will co-operate!

But, you may argue, how can I make the spirit of prayer prevail in my home without co-operation? Isn't co-operation necessary?

That depends upon what kind of co-operation you are considering. If you are thinking of the kind of co-operation you want, that is one thing; if you are thinking of how you can co-operate with what God wants of you, that is quite another thing.

For wives and mothers, the way to sanctity would be much easier if her family would co-operate. But suppose there is little co-operation, or none at all, or even downright antagonism. Will these things succeed in keeping us away from God when we know that He is drawing us to Himself?

In thinking about this, have you ever considered that these might be the very things from which God is trying to pull you away? That He may be trying to teach you to look first at Him so that in His reflection you may then see all those you love as He sees them?

This can be the first painful lesson in detachment that God is giving us. And it can be quite painful. It is not easy for us to realize — much less admit — that the wife and mother is not the beginning and end of her family, but only an instrument God is using to help carry out His much bigger plan for her family.

And so the second thing to remember is that we do not make any radical changes in our normal way of living. These changes may come later and gradually. They may not come at all. That is not important just now.

The important thing is our own personal co-operation with God. A change will take place, but it will have little to do with externals. The change will begin within our own soul and its effect will be in our own personal relationship with God.

As our own personal relationship with God becomes more loving and more intimate it will become increasingly easier to apply the effects of our own personal prayer to those around us.

Too often there is not much prayerful atmosphere in the home because everyone keeps waiting for someone else to start, with the result that no one gets around to starting. Many times there will be a sporadic start in family prayer when the oldest child starts Catholic school. But unless at least one parent is enthused about prayer the child will become discouraged about reminding everyone of something which should be an established good habit.

However, when our own prayer is as it should be, it will follow that the rest of the family will become less embarrassed about praying because we are not embarrassed. A husband who knows that the daily rosary is part of our schedule will more readily join the rest of the family in its recitation. When the morning offering is an established beginning for every day, it will be accepted — as will grace before and after meals, along with other little ejaculations during the day which are said spontaneously either as little acts of love or for special intentions.

Another thing to remember is that, for us, prayer must be more of a disposition than a regulated practice. In other words, the emphasis is not to be upon how many rosaries, or novenas, or other formulated acts of piety we recite in a day — although they may help if there is time to recite them. The emphasis, rather, is to be placed upon how we are doing all the things we have to do, in God's sight.

The whole idea is this: that we begin cultivating a prayerful disposition so that the *spirit* of prayer prevails every minute of our life. In this way we begin disposing ourselves to *live* our prayer so that eventually it will become a habit that is as easy and as unrestrained as breathing. We do not count every breath we take, nor wonder each time we inhale whether our breathing is keeping us alive! We know it is.

And that is how it should be with prayer. We should not only consider prayer as the lifting up of our minds and hearts to God — which denotes action on our part; we should consider it also as the breathing of the soul. Not the soul breathing with *my* breath though, but breathing with the breath of the Holy Spirit.

Going back to the natural plane we find that we do not stop breathing while we are working, or resting, or recreating, or entertaining or while we are doing anything else we have to do. Why then, should we be inclined to feel that the soul stops breathing while we are doing the same things? The only time the Holy Spirit stops breathing in the soul is when we choke out His breath with mortal sin.

The conscious realization that prayer essentially is not something we merely pluck out of our minds and hand to God, but rather His own Spirit acting within us to move us to pray, should be an immeasurable help in fostering the spirit of prayer in our own life.

MEDITATION

We should keep our prayer simple. If we try to reduce prayer to a kind of scientific formula — so much time for this kind of prayer, and so much time for that — along with a prodding curiosity as to how it all adds up, prayer will not do us much good. Our lives are complicated enough. The purpose of prayer is to make things easier for us. Unless our prayer is simple, we shall only add another complication to our life.

Take meditation. When it comes to active prayer on our part, meditation should be the easiest of all ways for us to pray.

But, you may say, for me that is the most difficult! I've tried to meditate and I just can't, my mind is always too full of other things.

If this is your reaction, then you have never stopped to really consider just what meditation is! Meditation is the easiest and most natural function of the mind. The mind is constantly considering some thing or another and this mental consideration is meditation. Often useless and destructive — but meditation nevertheless, on a natural plane.

The mind is inclined naturally to meditation. All we have to do is to substitute something profitable for the mind to feed upon and what was perfectly natural becomes now supernaturally profitable.

Of course, switching from one level of meditation to another is not always easy. It is easier for us to meditate upon our neighbors' faults than to meditate upon the Precious Blood which redeemed them. And the reason it is easier to meditate upon our neighbors' faults is because we probably know more about our neighbors' faults than we know about the Passion of Christ. So if we sincerely want to practice meditation as a form of prayer, we stop studying our neighbors' faults and start studying the life of Christ. And this study should lead to application.

The best way to start is with the Holy Sacrifice of the Mass. If we are sincerely seeking God, we most surely find Him in the Mass. For in the Mass we find the whole Christ. We find Him as the Infant and as the Redeemer; as the Wonder-worker and the compassionate Friend; as the ignominious Victim and the glorious King. We find Him as true God and true Man.

Finding Him this way we begin to understand that His infancy — even His incarnation — was the beginning of His Passion. Although we may marvel at the miraculous touch of His human hand, we realize that these miracles were but vague shadows compared with the miracle He has perpetuated in the Mass: the giving of Himself as our living food. We know that His compassion on the hungry of His time was stretched out over all time to include even us. We look for our hope in His glorious Resurrection, yet at the same time we never lose sight of the awful price He paid for His victory and ours.

As we seek God in the Mass, we find He gives us the whole Christ — the whole life and center of our Catholicity.

And then we consider what this Gift means to us. The Mass no longer seems a mere external form of worship but rather the heartbeat of the Mystical Body, the effects and fruits of which are flowing in our direction every minute of the day and night. We realize then, that circumstances which may prevent us from attending Mass do not stop the flow of grace channeled from the Mass in our direction. The offering of every Mass reaches out to include every member of the Mystical Body.

Volumes on the Mass could fill the whole world and still its facets for meditation would not be exhausted. The point in mentioning it here is just to offset the possible argument that there is little food for meditation in our busy lives.

If you have no other book of meditations, turn to your daily Missal and you will find something of Christ to set your theme of meditation for the day, and enough of Christ to carry you through a lifetime.

In meditating upon the life of Christ in this way we avoid the danger of lopsided devotion. It is perfectly all right to honor Christ in the Blessed Sacrament, or as the Sacred Heart, or through His most perfect Mother. What we have to watch is that we are honoring Him in spirit and in truth and not in the glow of our own emotions.

For example, we may become almost ecstatic in contemplating Christ as an adorable Infant — so Precious and so lovable — resting in His Mother's arms. And because this scene fills us with such a nice warm glow of emotional gratification, we become convinced that here is the devotion for me! We fail to see in this scene a foreshadowing of the day when that same adorable Body is lying bruised and mutilated in that same Mother's arms.

Picking out the scenes in Christ's life for the purpose of emotional gratification is hardly a fruitful way to meditate, but applying the whole of Christ's life to our life is.

For that is the twofold point of meditation: of fostering a prayerful disposition in our own lives; that conforming our lives to Christ's He may begin living His life in us.

SEEKING AND FINDING GOD IN WORK

MARTHA AND MARY

Working without a prayerful disposition is like working in the dark. Think, for a moment, how much you would accomplish if you tried to clean a bedroom in the middle of the night — with no lights on! You could work all night then find, revealed by the morning sun, a bedspread all awry, furniture only partly polished and dust still lurking in corners you hoped were clean. You would be thoroughly disgusted that so much effort produced such poor results.

If we separate our daily work from our daily prayer we are working in spiritual darkness. We cannot keep our spirituality in good order, we cannot polish our virtues and we cannot clean up the dust of our petty attachments simply because, in this darkness, we cannot see them. And when the Sun of Justice shines upon our soul at the moment of death, we shall be even

more disgusted that a lifetime of effort was wasted. The realization that the Light was there all the time; that we were too
careless and thoughtless to switch it on will be of little
consolation.

The perfect prayer is that which embodies adoration, thanksgiving, reparation, and petition. If our disposition is such that
the spirit of prayer is carried over into our daily work, then our
work becomes the living part of our prayer, for it can embody
all those things which make for perfect prayer.

It was thus that Martha served Jesus for she, like us, could
not sit at her Master's feet while the dust gathered and the
food lay unprepared.

*But, you may be thinking, even Martha complained! She didn't
like the monotonous drudgery which was her portion any more
than I like it!*

Yes, Martha complained. And most of the Marthas who have
come after her have been complaining ever since! But do any
of us really have a reason to complain?

Think a moment!

As wives and mothers, we are the Marthas in the Mystical
Body; that is the place which divine providence has allotted us —
a fact which we must admit joyfully, but too often we admit it
reluctantly and with dissatisfaction. Because we share Martha's
vocation we would almost convince ourselves that we cannot
ever presume to infringe upon the "better part" claimed by Mary.
Too often we turn away even from the desire for a share in the
"better part" because we take our Lord's words to Martha as a
statement of fact rather than as the reprimand He probably
intended them to be. "Martha, Martha, thou art careful, and
art troubled about many things: but one thing is necessary . . ."
(Lk. 10:41-42).

It could be that Jesus was not telling Martha that her activities were unnecessary or useless; or that she was wasting her
time preparing and serving meals. Being God, He certainly knew
about all the tiring, monotonous little things which make up

the big job of housekeeping. Being dependent upon her hospi-
tality at that time for the nourishment and rest He needed,
He would never have belittled her work with any show of in-
gratitude or lack of appreciation. What Martha apparently had
not considered, and what most of us fail to consider, was His
implication that she was wasting the *spirit* of her work.

We can hardly imagine the joy that should have been Martha's
in preparing and serving a meal to the Son of God, as she was
privileged to do. In that task alone should have been her joy,
her merit, her reward.

But what is she doing? Filling her mind with envious thoughts
of Mary; feeding her impatience with self-pity for carrying the
burden of work; possibly even banging kettles and dishes, and
then complaining that Mary could hear what our Lord was
saying and she could not. Martha could have listened to Jesus
too, *while she was working!* She could have heard every word
that Mary heard, had she listened in silence while her hands
were busy performing a service of love.

Martha was no farther removed from Jesus' presence than was
Mary, in as much as they were sharing the same house, even
possibly the same room. The difference was in their spiritual
union with Christ. Mary had forsaken many things to be near
Jesus; Martha had used the same things as a spiritual barrier
between herself and the Son of God.

Our Lord's words must have changed Martha's disposition,
for her feast day is celebrated on July 29. The fact that Martha
was raised to sainthood should be assurance enough, for those
of us who share her vocation, that she too was given a share
of the "better part." Legend does not imply that Martha retired
to the desert, as it implies that Mary did. We picture her rather,
living out her life joyfully serving others in her home, relishing
the "better part" even as she kept herself busy about many things.

A deeper conviction that Martha's way of pleasing Christ lay
in the humble tasks should be not only a source of consolation
to us, but also a real spiritual help.

WORK AS LIVING PRAYER

Have you ever thought that setting up the ironing board is the same as setting up a perfect atmosphere for prayer? Not the kind of prayer which would have us grasp the iron and repeat with grim determination an ejaculation or two — for we are considering prayer in a wider and deeper sense. Although we may hate the sight of the iron, being grimly determined to sanctify the task if it kills us — may do just that! It may make a martyr out of us, but it is not likely to make us any happier about the tons of ironing facing us for the rest of life.

And so the point in question becomes: how do we be happy though ironing, even though we hate the task?

The first thing we should do is to take the emphasis *from* what we are doing and place it upon the fact that we are able to do it, along with the hope that we shall be able to keep on doing it, whenever the occasion arises. And here already are two elements of our prayer: gratitude and petition.

No matter how much we dislike it, it is easier to be grateful for the ability to do the ironing than it is to be grateful for an incapacity which would need someone else to do it for us. Our ability to work is not a gift to be taken lightly, it can so easily be taken away. For then we could do nothing, not even the things we like to do.

Making a conscious effort to be grateful to God in all things makes it easy to adore and praise Him at the same time. Adoration and praise are only the homage we pay Him as His creatures, and we can adore Him in spirit while we are ironing as well as praise His goodness to us. It is as simple and as easy as that.

Needless to say, with this disposition, a despised task can soon turn into a loving work of reparation by which we help repair for our own sins and the sins of others.

And if you like to iron, all the better. Your ironing time can be turned into a loving meditation upon any subject you choose.

From the time we get up in the morning until we retire at

night, our whole working day should be lighted with this disposition — the spirit of prayer. It should pervade our every thought,
our every word, our every task.

*But this isn't always easy, you may argue, the daily grind of
housework can be a stark reminder of all the things I need,
rather than a reminder of the things I have to be grateful for!*

Do we have to fall into the trap of hating to make the beds
simply because we need new bed linens? There is nothing degrading about a patched sheet. It may not be as luxurious as a
new percale, but as long as it can be made to serve its purpose
a while longer, that is all that really matters. And if making the
beds with patched sheets still offends our sensibilities, then a
meditation upon the Son of Man who had nowhere to lay His
head, should make our own poverty more bearable.

That we should be grateful for the ability to mend, to sew,
to make things over, should not be such a soul-shaking revelation.
After all, these are the talents God has given us as wives and
mothers; humble talents perhaps, but talents nevertheless of
which we must some day give an account.

And so it should be all through the day. No matter what we
do, we shall find in every task something of God if we remember
to look for Him there.

Hanging up the wash can be an act of thanksgiving and praise
for God's beautiful sunshine and fresh air, making washday a
day of joy rather than of drudgery. And the rainy washdays?
They can become days of mortification; days on which we hand
over our will for the greater good God is accomplishing by
sending the rain.

Every time we drop to our knees during the day can be a
genuflection of adoration, and for the wife and mother this
occurs often: while scrubbing the floors, dusting under beds and
furniture, hunting for the children's missing shoes, or socks, or
books . . .

And the food you prepare for your family's meals — have you
ever stopped to consider in the light of prayer, the potato you

are peeling, or the pork chops sizzling in the pan? Do you think you can claim them as yours simply because you exchanged some money for them? The fact that you can claim them at all goes much deeper than a routine shopping trip. That potato and those pork chops were destined, from all eternity in God's Providence, to provide the nourishment you and your family need today.

How can we walk into a food market, look at the tempting array of fruits, vegetables, and meats without at the same time seeing the beneficent hand of God which has made all these things for us? Possibly we do not have as much money as we would like to spend, but we usually have enough. Suppose we had a fortune and walked into the market one day to find it empty? What good would the money be? It would provide poor nourishment if God's hand failed to provide the things we need.

These are little things; so small and insignificant that, in passing, they could be judged worthless and useless. But our lives are made up of little things. That is all really that God has given us and that is all that we have to give back to Him. In this light, then, every little thing becomes infinitely precious — not to be wasted, not to be despised; but to be exploited, in the spirit of prayer, for every bit of peace, for every bit of happiness, for every bit of personal sanctification which is hidden within it.

SEEKING AND FINDING GOD
IN SILENCE AND RECOLLECTION

We talk too much!

And when we are not talking we make use of every available means to keep the air waves vibrating with some noise or other — radio, TV, hi-fi. You would think, from our preoccupation with noise, that our very lives were sparked from it. You would think that there were some vital connection between the perpetual motion of sound waves and our own vitality; as though noise were a kind of generator which kept our physical and mental batteries charged; as though without it we would die — or go mad.

But silence is not necessarily death, it can hold the secrets of eternal life. It is not necessarily the negation of thought withering into madness; it can be the gathering together of the soul's faculties in the fruitful prayer of recollection.

For those who cannot bear the throbbing emptiness of silence there is little chance of finding peace in this life; there is small hope that the soul will ever assuage its restless desire for peace in the constant distraction of noise. And noise, as we are considering it here, is every kind of external and interior distraction: senseless chatter, our own or others'; useless thoughts entangled in too many useless things; distractions which scatter and dissipate the powers of the higher faculties like so many leaves in the wind.

The most devastating of all noise, it is well to remember, is not the clatter which pierces the eardrums, but the clever intellectual chatter to which we are constantly exposed, but which is nothing more than a cover-up for the shallowness of modern thought. Such talk is insidious because it is a constant preoccupation, usually, with what is lowest and basest in humanity; it is easy to become captivated with such chatter for it assails us on all sides in literature; TV, movies, advertising.

Even if we should plug our ears and cover our eyes, this particular kind of noise goes on and on, for it has invaded the very sanctuary of our souls. It has imprisoned us in a dungeon where concupiscent curiosity cries for more of the sensual food which will satisfy it, and the soul cries for the peace it cannot find.

We allow the dungeon of noise and distraction to build up around us — inadvertently perhaps — but we allow it just the same. We allow it, for subconsciously we believe that we will find our virtuous peace there. We become convinced that satisfying our curiosities as to what is base and perverted in humanity throws our own virtue into relief by way of contrast. We delve into the mud hoping to find our own purity and find ourselves covered with mud instead.

Instead of finding our true selves we find only our shame, and our shame lies naked before us, reminding us that we are cowards; afraid to indulge in the evils which so fascinate us and afraid also to try to rise above them.

And what has all of this to do with silence and recollection? Everything!

We cannot appreciate silence and recollection as the prelude to interior solitude until we get to work destroying the dungeons of noise and distractions. We must learn how, through persistent practice and determination, to eliminate all the external noises which we can control, and to ignore those over which we have no control.

Cultivating silence and the spirit of recollection is not the easiest spiritual exercise there is! It really does take practice and conscious effort at first. Learning to appreciate a silence which is pregnant with the presence of God calls for firm mental discipline. It is more than the snapping off of radio and TV dials; more than imposing silence upon others. It is the *putting to death* of all the idle vocal and mental gymnastics which may make clever conversationalists of us but which do nothing for the peace and welfare of the soul. It is learning to re-evaluate speech and thought in the light of Wisdom.

That we might learn, at least, the rudiments of silence and recollection, the opportunity of making days of recollection and retreats are offered us. Yet, have you ever observed a group of women making a day of recollection? It would seem, to most of them, that keeping silence means merely dropping the voice to a whisper. The resulting buzz of their silence is hardly conducive to recollection even though they may pride themselves that they have spent the day in prayer. Listening to their comments later you will hear them protest that there were *hours* (in chapel) when they did not even open their mouths. And mealtime without audible conversation was a trying penance indeed.

Closed retreats are better, at least the atmosphere of silence is more prevailing. However, closed retreats attract people who are more "spiritual," as those who can barely suffer through a day of recollection will testify. And so we are left with the impression that, although days of recollection and retreats are given to help us foster the spirit of silence and recollection thereby helping us incorporate it into our daily lives, there are very few who are really attracted to silence.

Why?

If we take the time to investigate, we hear over and over the common complaint that external distractions of modern living interfere with recollection, making it just about impossible to practice even if we feel so inclined. Yet those who complain the loudest are the very ones who will not give themselves over to silence when external distractions are removed — as they are during a retreat.

From this it would seem there is only one conclusion to be drawn: we do not enter into silence because we are afraid of it. It looks, to the uninitiated, like an empty, bottomless pit. We are afraid of it because we suspect that if our silence is quiet enough and deep enough we will meet God there and in the meeting come face to face with our true selves. The thought terrifies us. We prefer to hide behind the false premise that only a few are attracted to silence and recollection, and that we are not among them.

Yet there is not a wife and mother among us who is not inherently attracted to silence. We are as supernaturally inclined to silence and recollection as we are naturally inclined to companionship and conversation. We cannot be entirely happy isolated from social intercourse with family, friends, and neighbors and we cannot be entirely happy isolated from spiritual intercourse with God. We are made up of body and soul and we are happy only when there is harmonious balance between the two.

Our lives become balanced in this harmony when we begin to learn that silence — and the resulting recollection — is an interior state and not necessarily incompatible with external noise and distractions over which we have no control. Noise and distractions can, and probably will, plague us all our lives but with practice we can become their masters. We are not compelled to allow them entrance into our souls for as soon as we do, they become the masters and we become the slaves.

But you may ask, what about the distractions which seem to hold the mind with such tenacious persistence even in the absence of externals? When, for example, we come upon a quiet hour at home, or when we are kneeling before the Blessed Sacrament?

The best way to tackle this problem is to realize that there are distractions and there are daydreams. It is important to learn to distinguish between them.

The imagination is never entirely quiet. It flits around constantly gathering anything it can find, both factual and imaginary, from which it weaves and unwinds a continuous ribbon of ideas before the mind. This is the superficial activity of the mind. It has no real depth, and has no power over us unless we allow it to drag us around. If we allow our imagination to carry us away, then what were at first harmless distractions become involved daydreams. They invade the privacy of the soul. They fill up and disturb the silent domain which belongs to God alone.

The only effective thing we can do about distractions is to learn to ignore them. Once we learn to do this they will no longer undermine our spirit of silence and recollection.

Of course, if our useless daydreams remain more attractive to us than the reality of God's presence in the soul, then we will never learn how to be truly recollected. We will never learn to appreciate the wealth of spiritual treasure hidden in interior solitude.

If, on the other hand, we have ever been caught up — even momentarily — in the hushed silence which sings the wordless joy of being one with God, which stills the soul with a peace found nowhere else but in this silence, then we will see distractions and daydreams as they really are: nothing! Nothing to fear; nothing to cause concern: nothing worth exchanging for the peace of resting in God.

Distractions will certainly continue to come and go but as our silence becomes an interior habit, and our recollection more perfect, we will learn to ignore them more effectively. Once the soul has glimpsed the peace it seeks in the silence of recollection and interior solitude, the Holy Spirit will continue to draw it subtly yet ever more surely into that interior haven where the soul and God meet — and are one.

For this is recollection: being calm in the shining darkness wherein lies the peace of faith; being still in the tranquil silence wherein lies the joy of hope; being loved by God and loving Him with upturned face and open heart.

SEEKING AND FINDING GOD IN SOLITUDE

There are many people who prefer being alone because they like themselves better than they like anyone else. When such people withdraw from others they are merely indulging themselves, they are not seeking God in solitude.

Neither do the lonely know how to find God in solitude, for loneliness is nothing more than bitter disappointment growing out of the fact that they have never learned how to detach themselves from creatures in order to become firmly attached to God.

Interior solitude, then, is neither a haven for the selfish, nor an escape for the lonely. If we persist in interpreting interior solitude in the light of either of these false notions, we shall never come to understand it as the peaceful realm of the spirit that it is.

Interior solitude is at once a point of departure and a point of arrival; a point where the soul simultaneously leaves self and finds its true identity in God. In this solitary state we are given the first amazing glimpse of ourselves as God sees us, and we are left with a more certain conviction of who we are. And it *is* an amazing revelation. We find we are not merely a wife, a mother, or a person lost in the collective mass of humanity, but an individual stamped, by God's own hand, with a personal identity. As this realization grows, widens, and deepens, we find ourselves alone in God. We find ourselves alone, but not in loneliness, not in fear, but rather in the peaceful conviction of our true identity: the individual whom God has made like unto not one but Himself.

We come to understand that, in God, we are as alone as though He had created only us and no one else. With the deepening of this understanding, we find ourselves placed upon a solitary path, walking our solitary journey to God. With a conviction which is at once painful and reassuring, we know that we must walk this journey alone, our hand in God's, but accompanied by no other human being.

The conviction is painful because it is almost impossible for us to believe that we could ever go anywhere again — even to heaven — without husband, babies, children, and their assorted pets trailing behind us, or running ahead of us, or hanging onto our skirt.

But before God we are alone. We know it now as the truth; even though, inherently, we have known it all our lives. We have always known that at the moment of death we shall have to stand before God — alone — without anyone or anything into which we have plunged ourselves and in which we have felt rooted and secure.

In this state everything which before meant security to us dissolves into nonexistence, and we realize that security never had existed for us except in our own misconceived ideas. In the light of this new knowledge we find true security in our personal relationship with God. The reassurance of this truth fills our whole being with the conviction that we *do* belong wholly to God, and because we belong to Him, His care for us is loving, solicitous, personal.

We are consoled as He allows us a glimpse of ourselves in the new light of self-knowledge, for we see ourselves stripped of all pretense and subterfuge. This is how He sees us and we know this is how we must keep ourselves in His sight — walking in truth, without pretense of any kind.

Never could we mistake loneliness or withdrawal into self for interior solitude. Our first contact with this vast silence of empty simplicity broadens and deepens the meaning of solitude until it becomes a whole new spiritual domain. Within this domain the soul enjoys a freedom and unrestrained motivation that we may have heard about, but which we never could conceive as possible. The soul's movement is always in one direction: toward God. Although the soul seems drawn toward God, its movement is completely free and without constraint, as the rise of water seeking its own level is unrestrained; as fragrant smoke rising from incense, or as fire leaping from a spark.

This is the perfect solitude which the soul seeks; the solitude which attracts the contemplative to the desert. It is the solitude which only God can give to the soul and He gives it to those whom He will.

True spiritual, interior, solitude is infinitely more than a mere state of mind, its depth is such that it plunges into infinity — into contact with God Himself. It is as vast and overwhelming as any stark, unrelieved expanse of desert; remote as the most hidden hermitage. Such solitude is as silent as the star-studded midnight sky, as high and wide and deep as the universe; the infinite height, the infinite width, the infinite depth of God Himself.

In our daily living, in our vocation, and despite the intimate conjugal and maternal ties which bind us to husband and children, we must learn that before God we are alone. We must learn to walk in our aloneness before Him that we might begin to realize our at-one-ness with Him; that our soul might be attracted more and more toward interior solitude where God manifests Himself in silence and darkness to the soul.

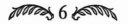

THE LIVING SPIRIT OF FAITH

May you be a witness to the essential values of this faith. Only God, the immortal soul and the truth and grace of Christ have absolute unconditional value. Everything else, no matter how high its temporal value, remains of a secondary order (Pius XII, August 30, 1954).

Every wife wants a faithful husband. Every wife with any common sense will cherish her own faith in her husband, her children, her marriage. Without such faith marriage is nothing but misery, even though this is merely faith exercised on a natural level.

For us who profess to be married in Christ, we need more than a faith on the natural level, we need a faith which has all the enlightenment and strength of a supernatural virtue. We need a faith which is vigorous and strong and which is centered, not exclusively upon husband, children, and the temporal advantages of the married state, but upon God.

If our faith in God lacks the vigor of strong virtue, our marriage lacks a strong spiritual foundation, for "Unless the Lord build a house, they labor in vain who build it" (Ps. 126:1). We would resist with our very lives any invasion which would threaten our marriage and all that it means to us. We are foolish indeed if we allow the blight of serious sin and the secularistic atmosphere of our age to invade and weaken our faith in God, and ultimately the very foundation of our marriage.

The supernatural virtue of faith, as it is infused into the soul at baptism along with sanctifying grace, is a living spirit — a living reality. Like the tiny mustard seed, having all the potentialities of the sturdy tree, faith contains vast potentialities of sanctity in time and of everlasting happiness in eternity.

We all have heard this truth reiterated often, yet for so many of us what should be a strong virtue is nothing more than an unproductive habit of mind. The married need the spiritual nourishment which faith provides; yet among the married, all too often, the living seed of faith remains stunted in growth; incapable of producing the supernatural fruits necessary for our spiritual nourishment.

THE BLIGHT OF APATHY DURING THE FORMATIVE YEARS

Serious sin and the materialistic age in which we live are, without a doubt, a double menace to faith. Yet if we take time to think about it, we find that they are not the real cause of weakened faith, they are merely the effect of our neglect to cherish faith as the supernatural gift of God which it is. In our youth we become so enthralled with the illusion of life and our place in the world that we forget that living in time is just a temporary arrangement. We become so preoccupied with living we forget that, in living in this world, we are also dying!

In examining why the blight of apathy infects our faith we must examine ourselves. As we take a look it does not matter whether we see the student as ourselves or as our children. We are all reflected in the same mirror.

And so we find that the undermining begins when we subconsciously start ignoring the importance of preparing to live for eternity and start concentrating instead upon the importance of learning to live in the world.

Catholics who have spent at least eight years in a parochial school have been given a good foundation in faith. The Sisters are conscientious and thorough, emphasizing religion as an important part of a well-rounded curriculum. During these eight years children learn their catechism. The Sisters see to it. They also learn the importance of prayer and the necessity of frequent reception of the sacraments as a safeguard of virtue.

By the time young people are ready for high school, they should be well started on the path leading to Christian perfection. The trouble is, they can also be well started on the path which leads away from God, complacent that they have had enough religious indoctrination to last the rest of life. At this age, the difference between learning the truths of religion and learning to apply these truths to personal living is something which does not sink easily into the head of a thirteen-year-old.

High school looks like freedom; freedom from so many of the things they felt they had to do. They begin dropping — without any qualms at all — so many of the things which appear to infringe upon this new found freedom.

Daily communicants among the high school crowd are few and far between. If you ask them why they will tell you that first, high school and daily Communion just do not mix. It means getting up earlier and that is a hardship. The second reason they give, and this would be amusing if it were not such a settled conviction in their minds, is that daily Communion is *strictly* for those thinking of entering the convent or the seminary!

Of course they have heard that daily, or at least frequent Holy Communion is a good preparation for any state in life. However, all too many have their own convictions as to what makes for successful careers and marriage; and daily Holy Communion apparently is not one of them.

They concentrate instead upon the "important" things. And so the exercise of faith for so many students, even of Catholic high schools, becomes hardly more than sporadic spiritual reading (required for book reports), occasional perusing of Catholic periodicals (again required reading), and the skimming over of a favorite prayer book, if one remembers to take it to Mass.

If weekly reception of the sacraments conflicts with the adolescent passion for week-end fun and week-end sleep, the former usually gives way to the latter. Confession and Holy Communion become a monthly, or even a once-in-a-while expression of faith, often to the dismay of concerned parents.

The apathetic exercise of faith becomes even more pronounced in those who attend public high schools. Their time in school is spent in anything but a religious atmosphere, so as far as their education is concerned, they seldom experience even an occasional nudging in God's direction.

With high school a memory, the adolescent steps over the threshold of maturity either to go on to higher learning, or to take a place in the business world. By this time all too many young Catholics between the ages of eighteen and twenty-two consider faith as nothing more than a secondary effect of their religion to be exercised only within the bounds of obligation.

This group scarcely ever offers its time or talents to parish activities. In fact any parish activity aimed in their direction is met either with cold indifference or downright opposition. They will not join discussion groups because they have their own ideas about "religion." They are not interested in premarital instructions because the Church is old-fashioned in her viewpoint on marriage. They will not make closed retreats, either because they consider the time involved boring and lost, or because they suspect that a retreat master's sole design is to snare them for the religious life.

These are facts. These are the facts which are a grave concern of parents today, but unfortunately they are our grave concern today because they are the same facts which surrounded our own growing up. Too many of us allowed the blight of apathy to infect our own faith and we have passed that blight on to our children.

EFFECTS OF THE BLIGHT UPON MARRIAGE

The apathetic blight which is a general threat to the vigor of premarital faith is real and its greatest danger is that it tends to obscure the divine end of marriage. The effects are already evident before courtship begins and consequently, for all too many, marrying another Catholic is more a happy coincidence than a serious and prayerful approach to marriage as a vocation.

The whole focus of marital happiness is centered upon finding one of the opposite sex who can arouse the emotions and passions to the highest pleasurable pitch of anticipation. Anything else seems unimportant. To emphasize to those who have fallen into this viewpoint that marriage is a vocation which obligates one to aspire to union with God could very well be met with the rejoinder that people do not usually marry because they love God, but because they love each other!

And so marriage and the pleasure inherent in conjugal love look like nothing more than a personal paradise independent of such accidentals as responsibility to, or dependence upon, God; responsibility to children and to society; responsibility for the spiritual welfare of the married partner; responsibility for personal sanctification.

Marriage may or may not strengthen faith. If faith is not much more than a sleepy mental habit; the accidental circumstance of having been born and raised a Catholic, the nuptial blessing is not likely to transform such a faith into perfect virtue. Granted that marriage is valid, and that there is faith in matrimony or in husband, or in children, such faith is no guarantee of everlasting happiness.

The reason is obvious, for such a faith has as its object a mere state of mind or fallible creatures, neither of which provides more than shifting foundations of sand, incapable of holding up the structure of interior happiness. There is only one real guarantee of happiness in marriage and that is faith in God. The virtue of faith is more than happiness in marriage, or the happiness dependent upon that which husband or children provide or dole out. Faith brings happiness of mind and receives and transmits its peace and joy not from accidentals, not from externals, not from creatures but from God Himself dwelling by grace in the soul.

Marriage in its early years can be such a private paradise, so gratifying, so completely satisfying that often there seems to be no reason at all to go to the trouble of exercising faith beyond obligation. The admission that God is good may be a little extra compliment handed to Him now and then, but since the natural plane of living seems to be a full and satisfying one, why bother with the supernatural?

Why bother indeed! Except when the first inevitable, painful cross of suffering, misfortune, or tragedy strikes, nothing in the natural sphere of marriage — or of existence for that matter — is able to fill the void of despondency and despair such an experience brings. No matter how much reasoning and rationalizing is done the answer to why such things befall humanity, and to what purpose, is left unanswered.

A weak faith widens and deepens the chasm of suffering. Without a knowledge of God and an understanding of His solicitude it is all but impossible to conform the will to His during desolation. If we do not know God well enough to love Him for His beneficence, how can we love Him for giving us a share of His cross?

EFFECTS OF THE BLIGHT UPON SUFFERING

The human intellect rebels against seeking the good in suffering, for to the natural faculty of reasoning there is no good in suffering. Yet suffering is humanity's heritage. It is the debt which must be paid for sin. Once we are born into the world, suffering is as much a part of our living as is growing, maturing, aging, and dying.

Anyone, plunged for the first time into the crucible of suffering may, in bowing to the inevitable, invent a whole litany of reasons why suffering may be good. But we cannot convince ourselves! The best of reasons will be hardly more than a self-applied counterirritant which does nothing except numb one misery with the application of another. Even though, at such times, the inestimable value of faith may be glimpsed; may be desperately longed for; may even be prayed for, there still remains the infinite gulf between repugnance and rebellion on the natural side and the serene joy of acceptance on the supernatural side.

Without faith suffering fights a losing battle against despair, for faith alone knows and understands the reason for suffering. The faithful soul knows that all Christians were born in Christ as He shed His Blood on the cross, and understands that Christians are perfected in Christ only in sharing His Passion by personal suffering. Without faith suffering is the beginning of a human being's destruction; with faith it can be the beginning of our sanctification.

Suffering can be our sanctification. By suffering in some form or other, we have our faith tested often enough, yet it seems that just as often we fall into discouragement and rebellion. Why, when our faith is tested in such a way does it not respond with the supernatural surge of sustenance we expect of it? This question can best be answered by trying to understand just what happens to faith because of indifference or neglect.

Through sanctifying grace we are given a share in divine Life, God's own life. In order that sanctifying grace might be the force propelling us toward God, it becomes active in us through the theological and moral virtues. The theological virtues, which have God as their object are faith, hope, and charity. These virtues are infused into the soul at baptism, along with sanctifying grace by God Himself.

Faith, the first of the theological virtues is an intellectual virtue; that is, its center of action is seated in the intellect. Since the purpose of the virtue of faith is to move the intellect to seek the truth in God, it necessarily follows that the seeking after truth must be a learning process. However, because learning or education can be a secularization of truth, the intellect may be drawn to seek truth in scientific, academic, or technical knowledge. Not that such knowledge is incompatible with the perfection of faith, as some would have us believe, but such knowledge can become a substitute for the truth which faith finds only in God. If this happens, the intellect may be perfected, but faith will suffer. Lacking intellectual nourishment and superseded by other intellectual interests, faith weakens as a living supernatural force and becomes simply an inert, unexercised habit of mind.

The habit of believing in God and assenting, more or less indifferently, to revealed truth along with the barest minimum of religious practices may be the only exercise faith is given. To expect such a faith to respond with enough strength to carry us safely over a crisis is about as sensible as expecting a sieve to carry us safely over a waterfall.

Although it is true that faith can be, and often is, revived by suffering, it is also true that suffering, once lifted, fades into unreality and with it the faith which temporarily sustained the sufferer. Although such intermittent "emergency" use of faith may be considered by some as its sole function; such faith is essentially weak and quite far removed from the purified and strengthened virtue which is the serene joy of the perfected Christian.

Faith was never intended by God to be a mere analgesic applied for the relief of the sufferings of His children; it is given to them that they may participate in, and enjoy an actual share in His divine thought life. In this sharing by faith, God's thoughts become our thoughts and we begin to see and understand all things in the true perspective of divine truth. This sharing in divine knowledge, though, will never become a reality in our life unless the living force of a vigorous faith becomes also an important part of our living.

For the married, the recapturing, deepening, and strengthening of faith can pose a problem. Ironically, the greatest obstacle in the way of perfect faith often is conjugal love.

This is especially true if such a love is sinful, as it would be if it amounted to a kind of worship which considered sin as nothing more than a legitimate part of that worship. This kind of creature worship not only undermines faith, it can be fatal to it. The more one creature tries to derive from another what only God can give, the more the soul languishes and sickens from an enforced diet of sensual pleasure. A faith directed exclusively toward a spouse may find a lot of good in its object, but it will also find disillusionment and frustration. It cannot find the joy and peace found only in God.

Another obstacle to the perfection of faith is sin. Since faith is one of the virtues through which sanctifying grace acts, it follows that a most necessary requirement for the perfection of this virtue is freedom from serious sin. Also since the virtues are perfected in proportion to the amount of sanctifying grace in the soul, it necessarily follows that the mere avoidance of mortal sin is not enough to cause an abundant inflowing of grace. The soul must also be rid, as far as possible, of habitual venial sin and of attachment to sin and to its occasions. In other words, although the fulfillment of obligation may keep us on the right side of virtue, leaning on the fence is hardly conducive to propelling the soul toward God. There is quite a difference between reluctant performance of duty because of obligation and joyful laboring because of generous love. All sin prevents the inflowing of grace into the soul but some sins put up a more effective barrier than others.

One such sin is spiritual sloth. Sloth has a way of being so habitually comfortable that the resulting spiritual torpor might be mistaken for genuine "peace of soul." Even though this spiritual lethargy may lull us into a false sense of peace, such a state bears a likeness to physical unconsciousness. An unconscious person may be considered peaceful, but he certainly could not be considered healthy!

Sloth has the ability to render faith unconscious in a number of ways: by providing all kinds of excuses, indispositions and convenient distractions when any kind of constructive spiritual program is suggested; by settling the mind in sleepy boredom whenever there might be a sermon to be heard, a spiritual book to be read, or night prayers to be said; by causing a discreet concern for the body which begins to languish at the mere thought of fasting or practicing any kind of mortification. Sloth discourages the soul from persistent seeking the treasure of faith with the conviction first, that even if the treasure is worth while, there will be an awful lot of laborious digging involved; second, after all that laborious digging, the treasure may prove worthless anyway.

Another reason why faith never advances very far is that it is kept watered down with too many human concepts and opinions. In other words the imagination goes to work constructing a notion of just what faith might, or should be, then works overtime trying to conform faith to fit the notion. When God tries to give us a hand by straightening out our notions, we lose patience with God because we like our own notions better. Thus our faith remains in a chronic state of strangulation because we persist in trying to re-make God into our own image and likeness. Our pride in our own convictions refuses to admit that God is beyond the finite realm of the human intellect; that He cannot be discovered in any production of the imagination. He is found only in the knowledge He has of Himself and that knowledge He transmits to the soul only in faith.

And then there are doubts. Many of us become discouraged and decide that we cannot persevere in seeking the perfection of faith because we have doubts. To some of us, having doubts seems to be the same as being a heretic and so, if we do not stop praying altogether, we at least avoid meditating upon the mysteries of faith by substituting thoughts which might be pursued more pleasurably and more safely. This is a grave mistake, for it is only by prayerful meditation upon the truths of faith that doubts are finally dispelled. Those who seek God sincerely and perseveringly in faith and despite doubts are rewarded by the interior light which God infuses into the soul and which is a participation of the knowledge and understanding which He has of Himself.

However, there is another kind of doubtful attitude which might be classified as a consolation, or a justification for lack of faith. Since these doubts are more of an indulgence than a distraction they are definitely more harmful. For example, we may experience a doubt concerning Christ's real presence in the Blessed Sacrament. Instead of annihilating the doubt with an act of faith, we follow the trend of the doubt into wishful daydreaming: wishing we could have lived in Christ's time; wishing we could have seen Him; or worse yet, wishing He would show Himself, or give us a sensible indication or feeling of His presence.

"O ye of little faith!" Even when the Son of God walked among men this reprimand was often on His lips. Even the visible proofs of His miracles were ignored by those who refused to accept His Word on faith. Immediately after satisfying the hunger of five thousand people with seven loaves and a few fishes, St. Matthew tells us that the Pharisees and the Sadducees came to Jesus asking Him for a sign from heaven!

Jesus' answer to those proud unbelievers stands as a challenge today as it did then: " 'An evil and adulterous generation demands a sign, and no sign shall be given it but the sign of Jonas.' And he left them and went away" (Mt. 16:4).

There is an awful finality in those words: *He left them and went away*. There can be almost heard in them His refusal to reveal Himself to any soul, even in the obscurity of faith, if that soul insists upon inflicting its own puny limitations upon faith. Faith cannot be captured, bound and placed within the limitations of human reasoning, for faith is a share in the knowledge of God which knows no horizons, whose depth is infinite and whose height transcends the universe.

THE STRENGTHENING OF FAITH

Faith, like any other living thing is strengthened by exercise, and the two most effective exercises for this purpose are prayer and the frequent reception of the sacraments. By prayer — thoughtful, reverent, constant prayer — the earnest seeking of God by faith begins, and the knocking is begun which will eventually cause the door to open. By receiving Christ in the Holy Eucharist over and over faith, nourished and invigorated, becomes the "fountain . . . springing up unto life everlasting" (Jn. 4:15).

For the wife and mother, as well as for anyone living in the world, faith must be a well-balanced virtue exercised exteriorly as well as interiorly. That faith revivified and strengthened by prayer, Mass and the sacraments does not remain a kind of private, secret, and selfish devotion; there must also be an intellectual or studious approach to its development. A life lived out in silence may never be called upon to make an open, public, or discursive manifestation of faith, but what married woman lives such a life? Every day presents situations in which a stand must be taken for, or against, faith. These situations range from the incidental questions posed by children, to the problems brought home from the materialistic and paganistic business world.

Can any of us living in this generation afford not to study the faith? Since life is one continual process of learning anyway, it should not be too difficult to add another subject! Lest the word *study* frighten those of good will, it should be understood that the study of faith does not necessarily mean accumulating a stack of theology works. Actually it can be very simple and easy, just by integrating the learning of faith into the other learning the mind is absorbing day after day. Of course it may mean foregoing a lot of the superficial knowledge toward which human curiosity is always being drawn, but as faith begins to come to life, such knowledge will seem less important anyhow.

Then too, in the process of learning, the most perfect teacher of all — the Church — should not be overlooked. Extra church services should be attended whenever possible, especially those which include sermons. The best instructive sermons are given during the Lenten season, during Missions, Forty Hours, and at special novena services held throughout the year. Joining discussion groups is also an excellent means of learning more about the faith as it provides the double benefit of listening and discussing. The Church is a tireless teacher, offering her children every opportunity to learn about, and appreciate the priceless treasure of faith. This teaching goes on uninterruptedly day after day; those who prefer to remain ignorant do so at their own eternal risk.

And spiritual reading should never be neglected! Most people who are afraid to open a spiritual book are likely to argue that they do not have the time. However, it is not likely that there is a literate adult alive who does not do some reading; one who is sincere in seeking Truth will find the time, even if it means cutting down on secular reading. Such reading should include the New Testament, The Imitation of Christ, the liturgy as it is compiled in the daily missal, the lives of some saints and whatever other books are recommended by one's confessor.

Do not be afraid to ask your confessor to recommend spiritual books which will take care of your own particular needs. In striving for the perfection of faith it is prudent to read only what the confessor suggests and approves. A gluttonous devouring of spiritual books to satisfy curiosity may very well result in spiritual indigestion which can be fatal to a faith not strong enough to digest such "meat."

TEMPTATIONS AGAINST FAITH

If there were a short formula for the perfection of faith, it might be contained in these few words: Seek God in spirit and in truth, and prepare for battle! The temptations against a strengthened faith differ from the doubts of a weakened faith only in their intensity.

It comes as a rather disconcerting surprise to some souls that a sincere seeking after God does not put an end to temptations. It seems rather unfortunate that those who write about faith; and those who define it and point with glowing terms to its advantages, its joys and its consolations, either minimize or ignore the trials inherent in the perfection of this virtue. In order that any virtue might be perfected in a soul, that soul must be purified and purification necessarily involves a certain amount of discomfort, if not outright suffering.

If more souls understood this, they might not take such a horrified view of their temptations; or be inclined to consider them as a sign that there is something essentially wrong with their faith. Nor would they hesitate to discuss these temptations with their confessors. Strong temptations which are vanquished are a sign that the soul is alive and is taking an active part in the battle against the world, the flesh, and the devil. A lethargic soul does not, as a rule, experience violent temptations for it usually succumbs without resistance.

It may be helpful also to understand the reason why God allows trials or temptations to afflict a soul. In sincerely seeking God, we find at first that God is delightfully sweet, satisfying, desirable. Of course God is all these things and infinitely more, but in the delectable glow of this new discovery, we are apt to be convinced that we have found a personal little corner of heaven. It is perfectly normal at this time to want to settle down in this enchanting environment and think that the storms have been quieted for good. Languishing in this atmosphere for too long a time, though, could be extremely dangerous. We would risk any progress we had made by falling into self-complacency, pride, and a host of other spiritual evils.

The danger here is that we would begin to think that we are entitled to such spiritual luxuries by being proud of our love for God, of our generosity, the multiplicity of prayers and devotions; in short, of all our accomplishments. Instead of being centered in God, faith would become self-centered.

Our Savior has said: "Not everyone who says to me, 'Lord, Lord,' shall enter the kingdom of heaven" (Mt. 7:21). After we say "Lord, Lord," for a while, God tests us to prove whether we are really sincere, or whether we are merely rendering lip service. The resulting aridity, lack of spiritual consolation, and the desolate feeling of being deserted by God can be very trying, but also very profitable.

To consider these trials or temptations as merely tests would be overlooking the most important part of their purpose. In this strange darkness of doubt and dryness is begun the soul's purification — the weeding out, as it were, by God Himself of the petty attachments and indulgences which hamper the soul's free movement toward Him.

If during these times we respond as generously as we can, allowing God to accomplish within us what He will, we will be drawn surely and safely to a more intimate union with Him. If we rebel, and persistently clutch for the straws of consolation we once knew and enjoyed, we will lose precious progress and even possibly, the most precious gift God would offer: Himself in a strengthened and purified faith.

THE DARKNESS OF FAITH

In order to live by the light of faith, the soul must enter into darkness. Unfortunately though, it frequently happens that in glimpsing the reality of this paradox, we shy away from the Light because we fear darkness. This darkness seems strange and terrifying; utterly new and unfamiliar, for it fringes upon eternity and within its depths is hidden the secret of eternal life.

It is a fact that a soul sincerely seeking union with God must travel through darkness. This is not merely a supposition; an accident of Christian perfection. This darkness is a spiritual reality, the truth of which is emphasized by every saint or teacher who has ever pointed the way to Christian holiness. Indeed, Christ Himself who is the Way, emphatically pointed out that there is no approach to the Father except through Him. Being hidden in Christ connotes something of what this darkness must be.

And yet, precisely, just what is this darkness of faith? Is it a frightening torment in reality? It may seem so in anticipation, yet if it is accepted with generosity and as a manifestation of God's will or — if you will — the price for a more intimate share in divine love, this tribulation is little or nothing in comparison with the peace and joy which is the reward for such suffering.

As this night settles upon the soul and envelops it, how can this darkness be recognized for what it is: the beginning or the continuance of the soul's purification? As a rule it cannot be recognized, at least not clearly, for the infinite variety of forms this night assumes is matched only by the infinite variety of individual circumstances with which each soul must work out its own personal salvation.

Any mother who has prayerfully watched a sick child lose its battle for life; any mother who tries to stretch an inadequate pay check to cover her family's needs; any mother who accepts another pregnancy as a gift from God when it could be a hardship; any mother who, because of a husband's death or desertion, assumes the double burden of raising her children; any wife or mother who lives her daily life as well as she can according to God's plan for her, enters into the darkness of faith. Whether this darkness takes on the proportions of a nightmare of desolation and desertion, or whether it seems merely a subtle semi-awareness of God's direction of her life, each time the soul enters into such darkness with a will conformed to God's it benefits by having its faith strengthened and purified.

If we could stand off and take an objective view of what is happening by way of increased sanctity during such trials, the crosses might be easier to bear. However, this vision is very rarely, if ever, given, for merit is gained and faith strengthened not in the understanding of the whys and wherefores of afflictions, but of the joyful acceptance of them in faith.

In his own inimitable way St. Paul describes this darkness when he tells us that "faith is the substance of things to be hoped for, the evidence of things not seen" (Hebr. 11:1).

His profound definition of the mystery of faith is in itself obscure, but a simple analogy may help our understanding of what he is telling us.

In the darkness of faith, we are hidden with Christ in God. Although sanctifying grace is the beginning of eternal life for us, the reality and the enjoyment of eternal life is not an actuality for us until we are brought over the threshold of death into heaven. So while we are awaiting the fullness of our supernatural life in heaven, our sojourn here must be in the darkness of faith. Thus the soul, quickened with supernatural life of baptism, yet hidden in God in the darkness of faith can be likened to the infant waiting in prenatal darkness for its entrance into the world.

Although thriving upon the substance of its mother, the infant nevertheless must wait until after its birth and after it is placed in its mother's arms before it can realize the actuality of maternal love. And so with the soul. Before it can realize the perfect joy of divine Love, the soul must be placed in God's arms by the angel of death. Meanwhile by faith, the soul possesses the substance of that which it hopes for — namely God and eternal life.

And again, what is more evident to an unborn infant than its mother; even though it cannot see her! Could anyone be so foolish as to insist that such a child has no mother simply because it cannot see her? By faith God becomes evident in much the same way to the soul, and it would be even more foolish to insist that such a soul has no evidence of God because it does not see Him.

Faith establishes a relationship between God and the soul which is infinitely more intimate than the relationship existing between a mother and her expected child; for the soul reposing in the bosom of its heavenly Father becomes one with Him; God dwells within the soul and the soul dwells in God. Thus it truly becomes a branch grafted to the Vine which is Christ, receiving its life from Him and bearing fruit in Him.

And the fruit of faith is peace. This is not the false peace which the world offers in the guise of materialism, secularism, in sensuality and self-love. It is the peace Christ promised when He said: "Peace I leave with you, my peace I give to you" (Jn 14:27). It has nothing to do with the world nor with anything the world has to offer, for it is not dependent upon the possession or enjoyment of material things; neither is it dependent upon any happiness or pleasure derived from creatures.

The peace which is the reward given to the faithful soul is the sweet unction of the Holy Spirit which softens and prepares the soul to receive the image of Christ, and which conforms the soul to live in the reflection of that Image — in purity of heart and in filial love and holy fear of its heavenly Father.

7

THE LIVING FORCE OF HOPE

Hope gives the soul that corresponds with grace the assurance of its future possession through the infallible promise of the Redeemer; it gives it a pledge, and as it were a prototype in the resurrection of the God-man accomplished at the dawn of a spring day (Pius XII, April 3, 1940).

Just because we happen to be exuberant, or inclined to hope for the best, or have an optimistic outlook for the future, does not necessarily mean that the supernatural virtue of hope is ours in any degree of perfection. We are all naturally hopeful; but only naturally. This natural hopefulness which moves us to seek food, shelter, and comfort is an instinct which we share with even the least of God's creatures. There is nothing supernatural about it. It is nothing more than the natural force which, having its roots in the sense appetite, nourishes the instinct of self-preservation.

A mouse can be perfectly happy scurrying around seeking those things which will keep it well fed and comfortable, but we are not mice! We cannot be happy with such preoccupation; at least not perfectly happy, because our supernatural relationship with God embodies a living, spiritual force which moves us to seek our ultimate happiness in Him, the source of all happiness. This living, spiritual force is the supernatural virtue of hope.

The human heart was made by God to find its joy, or happiness in Him and only in Him. It cannot find real and lasting happiness in anything else. If we persist in seeking happiness in creatures, material security, leisure, pleasure and an accumulation of years ahead in which to enjoy these things to the exclusion of God, happiness at best will be merely superficial. It will have no depth; no solid foundation. We may think we are just around the corner from happiness; in reality we may be poised upon the brink of despair.

The supernatural virtue of hope has God alone as its object. Since God is the source of all happiness, the virtue of hope enlarges the heart to relish the joy it finds only in Him, even in the face of temporal misfortune. Hope, as it is infused into the soul by God and strengthened by sanctifying grace, recognizes God alone as the soul's rewarder according to divine justice. Consequently it harbors no concern nor disquietude over the judgments, opinions, rewards, praises, or condemnations of creatures. Neither does it rebel nor despair over physical suffering or temporal misfortune.

Perfection of the supernatural virtue of hope within us is God's pledge of our happiness, which is only another way of saying that joy is the supernatural fruit of hope. However, we are not likely to perfect the virtue of hope in our soul by the mere pursuit of happiness. In the first place happiness — or joy — cannot become second nature to us until we understand just what happiness is and upon what it depends. In the second place, we must be determined to seek true happiness only where it can be found: in God, and refuse to be sidetracked by any false notion we may have been harboring all this time.

Happiness is not really elusive, it is just our false notion of happiness which makes it seem so. In pursuing happiness, unfortunately, all too many of us pursue a fantasy. We mistakenly seek pleasure for joy, and after having enjoyed — and tired of — one pleasure after another, find to our dismay that happiness has eluded us. In our ignorance, or in our willfulness, we cannot reconcile the fact that in the natural order happiness and pleasure have absolutely nothing to do with each other; that in the supernatural order happiness and joy are synonymous.

JOY VERSUS SADNESS

Every good force or inclination within us which would propel us toward God has its opposing passion or inclination to evil. Joy, the fruit of hope, is no exception. Just as peace, the fruit of faith is opposed by rebellion; and love, the fruit of charity is opposed by hatred, so joy is opposed by sadness.

Now obviously, in considering sadness as joy's opposing passion, we must make a distinction. This particular kind of sadness, which is an evil inclination, is not to be confused with sorrow which can be a holy and sanctifying emotion. Sadness, as we are considering it here, has its roots in despair; sorrow, when born in resignation to God's will has its roots in faith, hope, and love.

Theologically speaking, then, we find joy — or happiness — at the top of the scale of hope, and sadness at the bottom. We find further, that the law of joy or happiness of the supernatural order is fulfilled when the soul rests completely in God. Coming all the way down to sadness then, we find it is the total exclusion of happiness, for it is the passion diametrically opposed to joy. We find further that the law of sadness is fulfilled when the soul persistently flees from evil. The culmination of sadness is despair.

And here we must stop to make another distinction. At first glance we might be inclined to conclude that here are two opposing passions; joy and sadness, which employ the same means to arrive at different ends. This is not true, because by the law of logic it cannot be true. Obviously, we cannot rest completely in God without avoiding evil; that fact we know to be the truth.

But what about the evil from which sadness would flee? Is it the same evil that joy would avoid? It is not.

There are two kinds of evil: moral evil which is sin; and temporal or physical evil which is the effect of sin. They are both evils, but they are not both *evil* in the same sense. Moral evil is an evil state. In other words, anyone living and dying in the state of unrepentant mortal sin, lives and dies in an evil state. Such a person forgoes any hope of ultimate happiness; the joy of resting in God; the hope of heaven. This is the evil, and the *only evil* avoided by those who would be perfected in the virtue of hope: *the evil state of mortal sin.*

Temporal or physical evil, on the other hand, is not an evil state. Although these evils may range all the way from abject poverty to severe mental illness, and include all the miseries to which humanity is prone, these evils are merely circumstantial. They are the effects of sin, it is true, and they are real in that they cause misery, suffering, and affliction, but, in themselves, they have no power to engulf the soul in the evil state of sin unless we allow them to do so.

And here precisely is where we are inclined to get our sense of spiritual values mixed up. Our predisposition to sin would tempt us to consider temporal evils as evils in themselves. If we fall for that temptation, then we start falling down the ladder until we are engulfed by the sadness which sees no hope for happiness in anything except in that which the world has to offer. And so we become preoccupied with scurrying around like mice looking for the "things" which would alleviate our misery and provide some semblance of happiness.

Lost in this particular kind of preoccupation, the evil of sin may not even enter the picture. In fact it may even be employed as a means to avoid the temporal evils from which we would flee. If this happens, then happiness becomes ever more elusive. Despair yawns with the discovery that in trying to flee from them, we have been trapped by the very evils we would have avoided.

JOY HIDDEN IN SORROW

We are all afflicted with temporal evils in some form or other, at some time or other: poverty, physical or mental suffering, too much responsibility, too little recreation, failure, death . . . the list could be almost endless where individuals are concerned and where circumstances for each individual differ.

As we have seen, there is sadness which can be an evil inclination, and there is sorrow, which can be a holy and sanctifying emotion. When we consider the suffering and sorrow in which temporal evils can involve us, it would seem that these too, would be incompatible with joy. Where can joy, the integral part of hope, be found in them? Certainly not in the afflictions themselves for they tend to obscure joy — or rather any *feeling* of joy — in the soul.

This is an important fact to remember: that joy, the fruit of supernatural hope is not dependent upon *feelings* for its nourishment. It is nourished solely upon the "meat" of God's will. Take joy away from sorrow and you have despair. Consider joy as part of your sorrow and you have peaceful resignation to God's will. Here is where joy is found — in the soul's ability to rise above temporal evils and to rest trustfully in God.

There can be joy, then, in the affliction of poverty; for poverty is understood in the light of Christ's words: "Blessed are the poor in spirit, for theirs is the kingdom of heaven" (Mt. 5:3). Poverty suffered in Christ's name gives us, even in this life, a share of the riches of His kingdom.

Those who seek and find their happiness in God are able also to accept physical and mental suffering in obedience to Christ's counsel: "He who does not take up his cross and follow me, is not worthy of me" (Mt. 10:38). Christ accepted His cross joyfully for us; His true followers rejoice also in the opportunity to imitate Him by suffering pain and sorrow in resignation to God's will.

And who, living a life hidden with Christ in God is ever a

failure? In the eyes of the world, possibly! But in the eyes of God we are failures only if the final reckoning finds us condemned.

When God is the ultimate object of our hope, we remain strong under the burden of responsibility, because responsibility remains always well ordered. First in order is personal responsibility to God, then as God adds other responsibilities they are accepted and carried out as perfectly as possible according to God's will. Happiness thus is found, not in the love of responsibility, not in the perfection with which it is carried through, but in seeing in all responsibilities the will of God, and in God's will joy is hidden.

Boredom and restlessness from lack of recreation seldom, if ever, disturb those who find their joy in God. For them Christ's invitation to "Come to me, all you who labor and are burdened, and I will give you rest" (Mt. 11:28), is an invitation which is accepted gratefully and frequently. No matter what "refreshments" are advertised by the world, none of them can ever substitute for, nor measure up to, the spiritual refreshment enjoyed by habitually drinking from the living fountain of the Holy Eucharist, prayer, and mortification.

And although death may be looked upon by some as the most tragic evil which may befall humanity, for those who are steadfast in hope, death is their final victory. Christ has won victory over death, and so shall they for all the concupiscences which might have made death an evil have long ago been put to death. Having completely died to self during life, mortal death becomes simply a means of coming gloriously to life in eternity.

All this in theory is fine, you may argue, but is it at the same time possible in practice? Certainly, we want to seek our happiness in God and thereby avoid at least emotional involvement with temporal evils. But if we do, isn't there a danger that we may become cold, detached creatures incapable of compassionating suffering, of sorrowing over the loss of loved ones; incapable even, of enjoying pleasure? Who among us wives and mothers living lives so intimately bound up with others can live lives completely devoid of sadness, even though we instinctively seek happiness instead?

For the answer to all these misgivings, we need only remember that there is a definite difference between sadness and sorrow, as we have seen. A perfected hope does not guarantee an immunity from sorrow, but it does guarantee a supernatural immunity from the sadness which would lead to despair.

Consider, in this light, Christ's Agony in the Garden. When our Savior said, "My soul is sorrowful even unto death" (Mt. 26:38), He meant just that. If we could imagine anything cowardly about our Lord, we might presume to say that if His soul had been engulfed in the sadness of despair He would have been compelled to flee from His impending Passion. Make no mistake about it, when Christ accepted the bitter chalice from the hands of His Father, He knew what was in store for Him. He knew that His mortal body would be battered and bruised and pierced and finally given over to death. He was indeed a Man of Sorrows! Afraid, yes, even as we are over anticipated afflictions, but courageous nevertheless in carrying out the will of God.

It is only in the holy emotion of sorrow — our own personal sorrow — that we can truly compassionate Christ's sorrows and the sorrows of others. Only this kind of sorrow understands Christ's Passion as a Sacrifice consummated for our redemption. Such a sorrow also teaches us not only to unite our sufferings with Christ's, but to love and rejoice in sufferings for His sake.

THE MOTHER OF HOLY HOPE

Had our Lady's divine motherhood been lived out in sadness, that is in the preoccupation of fleeing from temporal evils, she would never have earned the title of our Sorrowful Mother. Think seriously for a moment of the infinite depth of her sorrows.

Do you think it was easy for her to welcome her God, her

All, her Son, in a *stable?* Think of her spending the years of her Motherhood silently adoring her Son — whom she knew also to be the Son of God — in spirit and in truth, while at the same time seeing those whose very lives He held in His hands ignore Him, despise Him and finally put Him to death. Could any one of us endure such a sorrow? And do you think it was easy for her, not only to share the ignominy of His shameful execution, but to stand at the foot of His cross, her heart breaking over His sufferings while at the same time being helpless to alleviate any of them? Do you think it was easy for her to echo with her broken heart, her Son's prayer, "Father, forgive them, for they do not know what they are doing"? (Lk. 23:34.)

"O all you that pass by the way, attend, and see if there be any sorrow like to my sorrow" (Lam. 1:12). What mother, before our Sorrowful Mother, or after her has even been, or ever will be called upon to probe again the depth of sorrow which was hers? Even a continual life of unrelenting sorrow would be only an infinitesimal reflection of her sorrow.

If our sorrows are the result of our own personal suffering, they are at least a small reparation we can make for our own sinfulness, while remembering that Mary who sorrowed most was sinless. If our sorrows are the result of the afflictions imposed upon us by our children, we know our children are mere creatures weakened by the wound of sin, even as we are. We can remember that Mary's Son was God — Almighty, Infinite, Innocent. The afflictions imposed upon her were the result of our sins and those of our children.

Do you wonder what sustained Mary in her awful sorrow? She was sustained by God through her perfect faith, her perfect charity, and her perfect hope. By her perfect faith she knew that our redemption was being accomplished by her Son's and her own sacrifice on Calvary. By her perfect charity her will was inflamed with the Love which not only offered this sacrifice to appease divine justice, but accepted it also, thereby reaching out to embrace all souls; even those who had put the Living

Evidence of her love to death. But it was her perfect hope which, soaring above her suffering sorrow, rested in the joy that all things were being accomplished according to God's will for the salvation of souls.

In the weakness of our imperfections, we could never plumb the depth of sorrow into which our Lady's soul was plunged. We can only pray that our sorrow will be, as it was for our Sorrowful Mother, the cause of our joy.

Sadness is pusillanimous, but sorrow is magnanimous. It is in the magnanimity of sorrow that joy is hidden, and true happiness is found.

THE ENEMIES OF HOPE

Modern secularism, which tenaciously tries to put respectability in virtue's place, is clever enough to provide attractive substitutes for individual virtues. In the case of the theological virtues, we may be tempted to substitute intellectual pride for faith; self-love for charity and presumption for hope.

Since presumption is absolutely incompatible with hope — that is with the supernatural virtue of hope — we may be inclined to ask how a soul could fall into such a delusion. It is quite easy! When we consider that, in the eyes of the sinner, presumption magnifies God's mercy to the exclusion of His justice, we come closer to understanding how we can thus be deluded.

If we are infected with the spiritual vice of presumption then we are like willful children who depend upon a doting mother to close her eyes against our misbehavior. We expect God to do the same thing; to close His eyes against our sins, yet have all heaven applaud the questionable good we accomplish. The more deeply presumption enmeshes us in mortal sin, the more we are likely to extol the virtue of hope — in God's mercy! This is all well and good, for if we are saved at all it will be because of God's mercy.

What is precarious though, is that the more firmly rooted presumption becomes, the more will self-reliance and self-complacency assert themselves. We pull our trust away from God and place it in ourselves. Instead of placing our hope in God and carrying out His will in our lifetime, we place our hope in ourselves, then try to stretch that pitiful hope to carry out our will in eternity. We fall into the danger of losing our soul because we try to inflict our will upon God during life; forgetting that in justice God's will *must* be done in Time and Eternity.

Despair is the most grievous sin against hope, for despair changes us from the image and likeness of God into the image and likeness of Judas. Despair begins eating at our soul the day we betray God's friendship for a paltry gain in material things, then find that these things are utterly worthless to exchange again for eternal life. Like Judas, a person fallen into despair is driven to throw away everything: the few coins which looked like a fair exchange for the Christ Life, and finally his own life which can no longer exist in happiness without Christ.

Even secularism avoids the mention of despair as it would avoid an unmentionable disease. It makes a lot of noise with words like optimism, exuberance, positive thinking, zest for life! But what are these but restlessness stimulated again only by the instinct of self-preservation? What can any one of these empty words do to ward off the despair which threatens any one of us who use them as a means to an end — the sole means in the search for happiness, to the exclusion of God?

When such a soul is writhing in its death agony, is the star of hope likely to break through the darkness to light the way to eternity? How can such a soul in its weakened state even see the star of hope, much less recognize it for what it is? Pleasure was the pathway followed; gluttonous pleasure, lustful pleasure, covetous pleasure; seeking always more pleasure, more wealth, more security in the hope that such things would bring happiness. The deathbed is filled with the dust and ashes of dissipation; leaving not even a straw of hope for a dying hand to clutch.

What is clutched instead is despair. And despair is hell.

THE JOYS OF HOPE

In considering the joys of hope, we must consider the temptations against hope along with them. This may seem like a strange paradox, but actually it is not. Obviously there cannot be much joy in battling temptations against hope; but there is an increase of supernatural joy every time a temptation against hope is vanquished. Without temptations against hope that virtue would never grow to supernatural perfection, and we would never know the joy of resting in the serenity of perfected hope.

And so temptations will most certainly stalk the soul who would sincerely strive to be perfected in the supernatural virtue of hope: and these temptations will take many forms. At one time we may be tempted to be cast down by temporal misfortune; to the extent even, that we be tempted to question God's justice in allowing these misfortunes to befall us.

And again, temptation in the form of disquietude may try, like a thief, to steal away our serenity by taking the gem of God's will manifested in the present moment, and placing it in a more attractive setting. Unless we are alert, such a temptation may cause us to fall into the delusion that God's will would be more perfectly carried out — and we could *hope* for better results — if we were living under different circumstances, or in another vocation, or at some future time when we feel more disposed to co-operate with God.

And of course there is always the temptation to despair. It may be subtle or fierce depending, apparently, upon the individual's desire for intimate union with God. During such temptations, the soul who finds nothing outside of God for which to hope, will at the same time find her hope battered with the doubts that she will ever realize the Object of her hope.

Although such temptations will necessarily cause interior suffering, we need have no fear, for the Holy Spirit will sustain and strengthen us — and our hope. The particular gift of the Holy Spirit which will fill the soul at such times is the gift of Knowledge which shows us the things of the world as passing vanities. The gift of Fortitude is also increased and acts in a special way to strengthen hope in the soul. By this gift we are given confidence that we shall triumph, with God's help, over the assaults of the devil and so come to the end of the battle without loss. Anyone who has ever experienced the supernatural surge of strength which Fortitude supplies, knows that this is not mere courage, but the very stamina from which martyrdom springs.

And since most of us are not called upon to suffer martyrdom; at least not the kind which severs life with one quick stroke, fortitude brings along with it patience and long-suffering. Patience: the refusal to be broken by sadness over temporal evils. Long-suffering: the refusal to be wearied by the enduring of affliction.

Any of us who may fear that happiness centered irrevocably in God is a negative thing, devoid of all the pleasures we would like to enjoy in this life, needs only to remember that the saint has the same capacity for the enjoyment of life as has the sinner. There is a difference though! A saint can, and does, enjoy wholeheartedly all the legitimate pleasures of life which God has provided; and in enjoying them her joy is increased because they are enjoyed in God.

The sinner, though, is inclined to seek her happiness in the illegitimate pleasures of sin — outside of God, and with the ultimate result that with the termination of pleasure happiness has retreated even further away. The saint has her innocent pleasures, her happiness, her joy, and her God; the sinner has her sins, her misery and nothing else.

Faith begets hope and charity sustains it; yet hope seems such an integral part of faith and charity that it almost remains hidden between them. Yet without hope, to what can a human soul be likened, except to a derelict skiff without direction or purpose; floundering helplessly in the engulfing darkness of despair!

Faith is primarily the participation of the knowledge and the understanding God has of Himself. Charity is the sharing of the love God has of Himself. And hope is happiness of heart. But hope, besides being the happiness which grows the more we anticipate the joy awaiting the journey's end, is also the star which guides us, the sturdy craft which carries us along, and the anchor which keeps us secure against the tempests and vicissitudes of the journey.

Hope places our hand in God's and teaches us to cling to the hand of our loving and omnipotent Father.

8

THE LIVING FLAME OF LOVE

*The first token of success in your apostolate will be your posses-
sion in abundance of this treasure of the love of God which
penetrates human love, develops it, sanctifies it, and renders it
capable, through the most humble signs, of reaching those regions
of the soul where the free and responsible person renounces his
pride, selfishness, and disordered attachments in order to sur-
render to the divine love which envelops him and leads him
forward according to its own designs (The Mission of the Catholic Woman — Pius XII — September 29, 1957).*

CHARITY THE VIRTUE

In our relationship with God, even though we owe Him
everything — our very lives — He does not compel us to do anything. He has given us the intelligence to distinguish good from
evil and a will to freely choose between them. He has made our
wills free and He respects their freedom. He allows us the full
privilege of this freedom even though we may choose to abuse
it, to our eternal regret.

However, in order that our wills might be more inclined to
become united with His, God gives us the gift of charity; the
supernatural virtue which, infused into the will moves the will
to seek God as the ultimate good above every other good.

Like faith and hope then, charity is one of the theological

virtues infused into the soul at baptism. Unlike faith and hope though, charity's presence in the soul is dependent entirely upon sanctifying grace — upon the absence of serious sin. Although mortal sin undermines faith and hope and may ultimately destroy these virtues, by way of pride and despair, the commission of even one mortal sin destroys the virtue of charity utterly and completely.

Charity is incompatible with sin for in essence, charity is a share God gives us of His own divine love. So it stands to reason that charity and serious sin cannot dwell simultaneously in the same soul. Charity in the soul is the verification of friendship with God. The charitable soul loves God and proves this love by always trying to avoid anything which would displease Him; the sinner loves sin and proves contempt for God by habitually defying Him and rebelling against Him.

Despite the fact that charity is the supernatural virtue which gives us a share in divine love, there seems to be a widespread misconception about charity — that charity is nothing more than *doing good*. Actually, in order to be perfect, charity does not really have to *do* anything! Charity is primarily the act of loving God; only secondarily does it become Love acting — God's love acting through us, that in the performance of works He may thereby be glorified.

St. Paul emphasizes this truth in his first letter to the Corinthians. In this particular digression on charity St. Paul lists a lot of things which could be grouped under the heading of "doing good," yet he dismisses them all as nothing unless they are motivated by the living flame of love which is supernatural charity:

"If I should speak with the tongues of men and of angels, but do not have charity, I have become as sounding brass or a tinkling cymbal. And if I have prophecy and know all mysteries and all knowledge, and if I have all faith so as to remove mountains, yet do not have charity, I am nothing. And if I distribute all my goods to feed the poor, and if I deliver my body to be burned, yet do not have charity, it profits me nothing. Charity is patient, is kind; charity does not envy, is not pretentious, is not puffed up, is not ambitious, is not self-seeking, is not provoked; thinks no evil, does not rejoice over wickedness, but rejoices with the truth; bears with all things, believes all things, hopes all things, endures all things" (1 Cor. 13:1–7).

Do you understand what St. Paul is saying? He is telling us that it is divine love which renders all virtues and all gifts fruitful. In the light of his meaning it is well worth the time to think more carefully about what he is saying:

"If I should speak with the tongues of men and of angels, but do not have charity, I have become as sounding brass or a tinkling cymbal."

Wives and mothers, as a rule, except those rarely gifted, are not called upon to deliver eloquent speeches. Yet St. Paul's words of admonition apply to us as homemakers just as surely as they apply to the lecturer. Without charity our words are useless chatter and our best arguments for good are as "sounding brass and tinkling cymbal."

This does not mean that those living in the state of mortal sin cannot communicate ideas, nor even extol Christian ideals. What St. Paul means is that words coming from a soul devoid of charity are words coming from a soul which is supernaturally dead. Although such words might have a supernatural effect on a listener, they merit nothing for the speaker.

When Christ came into the world he was the Word made Flesh. Although clothed in our humanity he was at the same time, the Word by whom all things were made (Jn. 1:3). This Word, who raised the widow's son from the dead, today clothed in the human speech of God's charitable ones, alone has the power to awaken sleeping souls and to give back life to souls dead in sin.

Even the silence of charity; the silence of those who love God, is more effective than the greatest eloquence of the hardened sinner, for the silence of charity is union with God.

"And if I have prophecy and know all mysteries and all knowledge, and if I have all faith so as to remove mountains, yet do not have charity, I am nothing."

There have been times when God has used extraordinary means to get His message across, but as a rule He uses the ordinary — the human instruments, such as we, to carry out His plans.

Our vocation as wives and mothers also includes the role of teaching. This seems to be the meaning St. Paul gives to the word *prophecy* when he says ". . . he who prophesies speaks to men for edification, and encouragement, and consolation" (1 Cor. 14:3). It follows, then, as God's ordinary instruments, that it is our responsibility always to be his worthy instruments.

Without charity's illuminating grace we are not likely to be inspiring teachers of God's law. And without charity — living in the state of sin — all the preaching we may do will merit nothing for ourselves. It follows also, that we cannot teach our children to love God and appreciate the things of God if we ourselves are not loving God as perfectly as we should.

Just as Christ is the Word by which all things were made, so also is He the "true light that enlightens every man . . ." (Jn. 1:9). Christ's light remains in the world in the supernatural virtue of charity. His torchbearers are those who are charitable of heart.

"And if I have all faith . . ."

Faith without charity is like a map without a journey. No one will argue that we can learn how to go from here to Mt. Everest by sitting in an armchair and studying a map. In this way we can learn everything we need to know about the journey, but the map will never fulfill the purpose for which it was printed unless we get up from the armchair and undertake the journey. A map in itself is not a journey, and faith in itself is not salvation.

We may believe everything our faith teaches; we may go through life without harboring the slightest doubt concerning any of the mysteries of faith, but unless charity unites our will to God's and supplies the impetus to carry out God's will for our personal sanctification, our faith is nothing at all.

"And if I distribute all my goods to feed the poor, and if I deliver my body to be burned, yet do not have charity, it profits me nothing."

We might be inclined to argue with St. Paul over this particular statement. Most of us are convinced that giving all one's goods to the poor would be heroic charity. Yet St. Paul says that this is not always so. And the reason this is not always so is that we could give all our goods to the poor from a natural motive as well as from a supernatural motive. Natural motives as a rule have little or no merit in God's sight.

For example: a man might give everything he has to the poor because tomorrow he is being electrocuted. In doing this he is acting from a natural motive since he knews that tomorrow he will no longer need his possessions. Although the poor may benefit from this gift, the condemned man can hardly claim merit for his "charity," since it is unlikely he would be so generous if he knew that tomorrow he would be pardoned!

Incidentally such a man would also be giving his body to be burned, but because he is doing so in penalty for serious crime, he is not likely to be canonized. In fact, if he goes to the electric chair unrepentant, he will not be numbered among the blessed in heaven. Only one who embraces poverty for the love of God grows in charity; only one who gives his life for Christ becomes a martyred saint.

St. Paul goes on to tell us that "charity is patient." The reason that charity is patient should be obvious; for what is impatience but an external manifestation of pride, and what is pride but the stubborn hardness of self-love — charity's worst enemy.

Only the proud are impatient; the humble never are; for the proud love themselves and the humble love God in charity. Impatience is the soul's restless rebellion against the restraint of self-love; patience is the serene freedom enjoyed in the infinity of divine love.

"Charity . . . is kind . . ."

Kindness is the overflow of love, for kindness is love's tender ministration. Only hatred deliberately inflicts injury for hatred seeks satisfaction in destruction. The kindness which emanates from supernatural charity seeks always to repair, to help, to uplift, and to strengthen and does all these things with loving tact.

"Charity does not envy . . ."

The gaze of charity embraces the whole of God's world and finds no one of which to be envious. Envy which exults over another's adversity; or which would belittle another's success, lies vanquished at charity's feet. The charitable soul possesses God, the Source of all riches, all joy, all peace and contentment so what, possessed by another creature, could charity desire?

"Charity is not pretentious, is not puffed up, is not ambitious, is not self-seeking, is not provoked."

Charity scorns these vices for they are the malicious vices of self-love. The simplicity of charity could never in truth pretend to be what it is not; the humility of charity recognizes and accepts the creature's relationship to her Creator and finds nothing in herself of which to be proud.

The ambitious person seeks her own glory, or the glory of others that she may bask in their reflection; charity's only ambition — if it can be called an ambition — is the desire to love God perfectly and to help others realize the joy of this love.

Neither is charity self-seeking, for charity labors ceaselessly for no other reason than to carry out the will of God in her own life, and to bring the Kingdom of God into the lives of others.

And so neither is charity provoked, for the charitable are the peacemakers who are the children of God; the meek who shall someday possess the land.

"Charity . . . thinks no evil . . ."

Since true love is never suspicious and avoids thinking evil, at least of the one loved, charity the only true love there is, does not deliberately think evil of anyone. This is not because charity is blind in the sense that love is said to be blind; rather it is because charity has the penetrating vision to see beyond the evil of sin and find the image of God — and thus the good — in every soul. Because charity rejoices only in the degree of perfection of the divine image in a soul, it cannot rejoice over wickedness. Wickedness causes the charitable to sorrow, for wickedness not only obscures the beauty of souls, it also impedes the work of love in the world.

"Charity bears with all things . . ." in order that God's will may be done; "hopes all things" will carry out God's will, and "endures all things" for the love of God and for the salvation of souls.

If we take St. Paul's words seriously we should never forget that any of the spiritual or corporal works of mercy are merely external effects of charity. They are but small drops of water in comparison with the ocean which is the supernatural virtue of charity. If they spring from a zeal which would ease a guilty conscience, they are nothing but drops of water sprinkled on a bonfire!

GROWTH AND PERFECTION OF CHARITY

Although sanctifying grace is the spiritual soil into which charity plunges its roots, the mere absence of mortal sin does not presuppose the perfection of charity. The absence of mortal sin merely disposes our soul for a greater infusion of charity. Abandoning sin is the first step. Realizing the perfection of charity is a gradual ascendance or growth, dependent upon many successive steps taken in the direction of God.

Every time our will embraces God instead of sin our soul receives an increase of charity. Whether this choice of God is the result of victory over temptation, or whether it is a turning back to Him after having fallen into sin, the fact that we have freely chosen God causes the supernatural virtue of charity to grow and thrive in our soul. In thus acting we prove that we love God and so dispose ourselves to receive a greater measure of His love.

Charity then, is the soul's crowning virtue of perfection, but it is perfected only in as much as all the other virtues are perfected. In the beginning, the work of cultivating and perfecting charity is divided. Some of the work we do, some of the work God does for us. Our work consists primarily of avoiding sin, of ridding ourselves of obvious faults, of forming good habits to take the place of bad ones. God responds to our efforts by facilitating the practice of virtue and by granting sufficient grace to overcome temptation and persevere in His love.

In this way we become more and more disposed to receive an ever greater measure of God's love. As this measure of love increases, charity within the soul becomes less our love for God and more God's love for Himself. As charity begins flooding our soul with divine love, each act of responsive love will dispose our soul for an ever greater measure of divine love.

A word of caution may be wise here, just in case there may be an inclination to place an overromantic emphasis upon love — especially upon divine love. The virtue of charity is not a vague kind of sublime emotion in which the soul constantly and ecstatically enjoys God! Any pleasant emotional feeling of affection for God that we might experience now and then, may be a grace spurring us on to practice charity more perfectly, but it is not the virtue of charity itself. It cannot be emphasized too strongly nor too often, that charity is not an emotion but rather, being a virtue it is a power to act. Or more simply, it is love acting.

Anyone who is familiar with the action of love, as every wife and mother should be, knows that love acts primarily to please the one loved and secondarily to increase the bond of love between those who love each other. For those who love each other the happiness, or the perfection of love, must be a well-balanced activity of give and take.

During the progressive perfection of charity the same truth holds. The intimate relationship between the soul and God must be regulated by this same well-balanced activity. In order that charity might be perfected in our soul we cannot sponge upon God's generosity, even though that generosity is boundless, without giving Him something in return; and neither can we presume to be so generous with God that we refuse to take anything from Him.

One extreme can be as dangerous as the other. Love is such a gratifying emotion that it can tempt us to seek love primarily for the gratification it gives. This is true in the natural order and it can be dangerously true in the supernatural order, especially for those who really want to love God, but more for what He can give than for what He might expect. The individual who loves creatures, whether they be husband, children, or friends simply to enjoy emotional gratification is inclined to love God in the same manner. The person who suffers — and suffer she must — from this disordered conception of love can never hope to be perfected in supernatural charity unless she learns to evaluate love not only in terms of taking, but also in terms of giving.

If we desire a share of divine love merely to keep us satisfied, and gratified and pacified in a sensual kind of way, we shall never be perfected in charity. Since there is nothing sensual in the pure spirituality of divine love, our souls will never arrive at enjoying the fruits of perfected charity if we try, for example, to replace frustrated sensual* love with divine love. Charity, or love of God, cannot ever be a "substitute" love, that is a love used to fill up the void caused by a disappointment in human love. It is impossible to love God perfectly simply because we have discarded the love of a creature, or creatures, and feel the need of someone to take their places.

We may turn to God because our husband has been unfaithful, or because our children have deserted us, but we cannot expect Him to fill us with an ecstasy which will make our hatred for them more bearable!

---

* By sensual love is not necessarily meant illicit love. What is meant is any kind of inordinate love which is sought simply for self-gratification, whether it be sought in husband, children, or others.

In this extreme, or even on the dangerous fringes of this extreme, we have a good example of the soul who would seek to love God simply for what she might obtain from Him. Even though such a soul may sincerely believe that she has abandoned herself to divine love; even though she may feel that her particular case justifies her looking to God for the consolation she feels she deserves for those who have injured her past the point of forgiveness — she is only deluding herself.

God will console her, yes — as He consoles every one of us who take our disappointments and frustrations to Him. But such a one cannot hope to be perfected in charity unless she can be generous enough to give God not only her own soul, but also the souls of those who have injured her; and give them with loving trust to His loving care. God is love and in order to become acquainted with Him as the Lover of our soul we can find Him only in pure love; never in a love which would be only a salve for bitterness or hatred.

Charity is not all giving *either!* If we become enamored with the notion that charity is nothing more than the precept. "It is more blessed to give than to receive," we are apt to rush headlong into battle determined never again to receive, but only to give! Needless to say, our defeat can be even more ignominious than the defeat suffered by the timid selfish. Rash, tactless, and boorish generosity can throttle supernatural charity in the soul as thoroughly as can a kind of furtive charity practiced for self-gratification.

We must guard against this dangerous extreme in our relationship with God; and we must guard against it in our charitable relationships with our neighbor.

DANGERS OF RASH GENEROSITY

RASH GENEROSITY TOWARD GOD

"It is better and safer for you to conceal the grace of devotion, not to be elated by it, not to speak or think much of it, and instead to humble yourself and fear lest it is being given to one unworthy of it" (*Imitation of Christ*, Bk. 3, c. 7).

We cannot impress God with our generosity because in the first place we are not very generous, and in the second place whatever generosity we may have, God Himself has given us. So although we may think we are strong enough to do heroic things for God, we must constantly guard against the rash generosity which would subconsciously seek to impress Him.

For example we may say to God: "I give You my life; and in order that I may love You perfectly I beg You to do with me what You will."

Since God has an infinite number of ways of responding to such acts of love and generosity, it would be presumptuous to say just how He may respond. As a rule though, if we make such an act, we will be aware of God's response and with this awareness our generosity is usually put to the test. When this happens we must make the decision as to whether we want a more intimate relationship with God by accepting whatever He offers, or whether we will withdraw a generosity which is not strong enough to support the words it professed.

No matter what God asks, if our response is: "Not my will, but Thine, be done," He will grant us the grace of perseverance. A rash generosity, though, will shrink from His demands with the excuse that "although I want to go all out in generosity with God, I prefer that He would not be so generous with me!"

In so many words we tell Him to give His cross, His special blessings, the graces of tribulation or interior suffering to His chosen few and leave us the things which are easier to bear. Striking our breast with feigned humility we say, "Behold the handmaid of the Lord — but I am not worthy to be one of Your saints!"

And since God will not force even His gifts and His love upon us against our will, the treasures He had in store for us remain unused.

Rash generosity is nothing more than a manifestation of pride; the exaggerated sense of our own perfection — self-love. A generosity prompted by such pride is like a sealed cover which we keep on our hearts, preventing them from being filled with the infinite bounty of God's love.

Trying to get for ourselves a share of divine love by means of such a generosity is like trying to get a drink of water with a covered cup. The flowing water could splash upon the closed cup forever — while we die of thirst. And we die of thirst, not because of the scarcity of water, but because of our own stupidity!

And so it is with charity, unless we open up our hearts that God may fill them with His love, our charity will never be increased, even though we beg Him for charity all our lives.

But with hearts uncovered and emptied that is, purified from all self-love and attachments, who can judge the measure of charity God has willed for any one of us? God's love is infinite and He wills to share it with us; full measure and as much as we can hold. Who could presume to say that He does not will a heroic degree of charity for each of us?

Yet there are those who seem to be perplexed by this very problem. They would presume to measure God's generosity by the absence of charity in the world; or by the lack of their own generosity. They point to evil's ascendancy as though it were a failure on God's part to provide sufficient grace to enable evil to be overcome. They overlook the obvious cause: humanity's lack of humble generosity; humanity's willful rejection of the graces God offers.

We may rest in the false complacency that sanctity is not for us; that it is only for a chosen few, but can we truthfully say that God does not will holiness for us? If we do, our complacency might be due for a horrible jolt when we find in the light of eternity that God may have reserved for us as high a degree of glory as He had for — say, the Little Flower. It may be to our eternal confusion to realize that the reason why we did not rise to St. Therese's height was because she utilized every grace God offered her, while we picked and chose only those we thought might work to our advantage.

The greatest torment of remorse suffered in eternity either in purgatory or in hell is the realization of the graces discarded in a lifetime; either because of a rash generosity which could not make good its boasts, or no generosity at all.

RASH GENEROSITY TOWARD OUR NEIGHBOR

One of the most familiar examples we have to illustrate this danger is the matron who decides to be charitable by giving some of her time and money to help the poor. Determined to be charitable at all costs, she ventures forth to inflict her generosity upon her victims. She has no particular love for the poor but she is determined to be charitable. Their squalor and apparent lack of self-respect torment her sense of delicacy, but her repugnance merely proves to her the perfection of her virtue.

And the results of her campaign? The poor become more miserable! Added to their former misery is their humiliation of feeling obligated to one who doles out favors as she might administer castor oil — for their own good! If they were not so hungry they would probably give into the temptation to throw her gifts in her face. Even the warmth she may provide for their rooms fails to warm the chill of resentment she leaves in their hearts.

Meanwhile she, who was so gratified at first by the warm glow her new charity fired, finds frustration rather than satisfaction gaining the upper hand. These poor! They have proved only what she has known all along. There is no gratitude among them for all she has done out of the goodness of her heart.

Whatever spark of charity she may have had has long since died and for the poor now, she has nothing but contempt.

Yet someone else may knock on the door of these same poor and leave them not only material gifts, but also new hope and joy. The person who really succeeds in alleviating the misery of the poor is the one whose charity has all the graciousness, all the tactfulness, all the warmth of divine love. She knows that in giving to the poor, she must also receive something from them. The poor may be happy that she has taken from them a cup of hot tea, or a wilted flower from a grimy little hand; but actually she received more than this.

When she came to them she offered them not her generosity but Christ's love acting through her and emanating from her. When she left them she had received an increased measure of love — for in bringing Christ to them, she found Christ waiting for her in them — and love leapt up to unite her and the poor as one in Christ.

The person whose love of God is nothing more than a form of self-love manifested in rash generosity, can neither love God above all things, nor can she love her neighbor as herself. Consequently such a person has small chance of being perfected in charity, because she loves herself above all things and despises the neighbor who can never measure up to the opinion she has of herself.

We cannot, as a rule, recognize the image of Christ in others until we have become familiar with the reflection of Him in our soul. Unless Christ is enthroned in a human heart, He cannot rule even a small part of His Kingdom through that human heart. Unless we first possess Christ in charity we cannot even presume to give Him to others. Unless the fire of divine love, which is supernatural charity, is a strong, constantly burning flame dispelling the darkness in our own soul, we cannot hope to share this love with others.

CHARITY'S WORST ENEMY

We cannot hope to vanquish an enemy unless we recognize it; nor can we avoid an attack if, in watching over the wrong places, an enemy sneaks through an unguarded opening.

The enemy of charity is not found in the people who try our patience; neither is it found in the confining duties which have an irritating way of keeping us from doing big things for God. Nor do we find charity's enemy in the straitened circumstances which might prevent us from being as generous as we think we would like to be toward God's poor. All of these things combined to make up our own God-given circumstances, are merely incidental so far as charity goes. Not one of these things, nor any combination of them can affect charity at all unless the true enemy of charity is doing the undermining.

Charity's worst enemy is selfishness, or self-love because self-love would have us try to make our life the center of love instead of recognizing charity as the center of our life. Under the impetus of self-love, we not only desire to be loved, we expect it, since we consider ourselves to be completely lovable. If our lovableness were more a fact and less an opinion, we might be more disposed to grow in charity. As it is, selfishness sets up love in the wrong place — within ourselves, instead of centering it in God, the source of all love.

Being diametrically opposed to charity, self-love is a disordered love spreading poison not only among those with whom we live, but among those with whom we come in contact. Selfishness makes of us a shell in which love would be held captive even though we know an imprisoned love is not conducive to happiness. In fact, the selfish wife is fortunate indeed if her marriage or her motherhood make her even reasonably happy.

Self-love, or self-centered love can be such a pleasant substitute for charity that often it is the sole preparation for marriage. When this is the case, such a love views marriage as nothing more than a perpetuation of ecstatic thrills, expensive presents, and extensive adulation. Gratification is all that it wants from marriage.

Carried over into marriage, such a love will first obscure, then try to avoid the responsibilities of marriage. Since selfishness is a gluttonous thing demanding always to be satisfied, hardships serve only to aggravate its appetite and if it cannot avoid them, it will fold up under them in the manifestation of neurotic or psychotic disorders.

Substituted for charity in marriage, selfishness causes everyone to suffer. The husband suffers because it is impossible to meet the demands of such a love either emotionally or financially. The children suffer because they cannot measure up to the ambitions projected upon them. The wife suffers most of all because in trying to keep love captive within herself, she inadvertently puts love to death.

This self-love is evident in varying degrees in the brittle career wife; in the socially ambitious wife; in the jealous or suspicious wife; in the discontented or nagging wife; in the wayward wife and often in the abandoned wife. It is evident also in the possessive mother, the ambitious mother, and in the negligent or the neglected mother. Surprising enough, it may also be the force behind the zeal of the tireless parish worker, the organizer, and the self-appointed apostle.

Wherever this self-love is evident it brings along with it a whole bevy of vices: including malice, boasting, discord, contention, falsehood, detractions, calumnies, indignation, agitation, and even violence and strife. Those of us who are guilty of any of these vices are guilty of the same thing: a selfish love which would gorge itself upon the generosity, the esteem, and even the love of others while giving them nothing in return.

This is how we would mistakenly make our life the center of love, as though love were our just due; as though we deserve it simply because we are the lovable persons we think we are — despite our glaring faults! If this is our ambition, we are nothing but foolish, deluded creatures destined at least to be pitied, if not despised by everyone unless we learn the true meaning of love hidden in the virtue of charity.

Love can never be centered in ourselves because it is irrevocably centered in God; we cannot draw love to ourselves unless our misery draws upon God's mercy and floods our soul with

His divine love. Only in this way does love become the center of our life. From this center love will gradually grow and expand, if we are careful to tend its growth and give it room for expansion.

Charity, then, is not only the virtue which assures our eternal salvation, it is the virtue which also assures a fruitful and happy marriage, because it is charity which perfects love. Charity lifts our puny, selfish love above the plane of mere emotional involvement and places it in its true environment, the boundless infinity of divine love.

APPLIED CHARITY

In every marriage the time inevitably comes when charity must be applied to heal the wounds inflicted upon us by the disillusionment and disappointment springing from the imperfections of human love. Within charity is hidden the secret of spiritual health which alone helps us build up a holy immunity for ourselves and preserve the healthy sanctity of our marriage. It is the degree of our own charity which supplies a necessary degree of forbearance, patience, understanding, and kindness. These in turn act as spiritual buffers which protect the integrity of our own soul and the integrity of our marriage.

The trouble with most of us, though, is that we are inclined to latch onto the irritations of married life and exaggerate them, instead of latching onto charity and cultivating it.

We all have faults. That is one truth none of us deny. However, despite our faults we are at the same time perfectionists, and born reformers! We expect everyone and everything to measure up to our own idea of perfection; including our husband and our marriage. For some reason we insist upon clinging to the conviction that there is nothing wrong with our marriage that a perfect husband would not remedy. We are inclined to overlook the obvious truth that besides a perfect husband, a perfect marriage also needs a perfect wife!

And a perfect wife is not necessarily an injured wife. All too often her injury is only the result of her neglect or refusal to apply charity when and where it was needed.

How many of our priests leave the confessional burdened with sorrow over the gaping and festering wounds evident in so many of our marriages! Especially when a parish mission opens the floodgates of those souls who are apparently hardened to marital misfortunes. Among the married the confessions usually balance out. Wives complain of unfaithful husbands; of drinking husbands; of irresponsible husbands. Husbands complain of suspicious wives; of ambitious wives; of nagging wives.

Why isn't the healing touch of charity applied before the damage is done? Would the unfaithful husband have taken that first step in the wrong direction if his wife's love had been strong enough in charity to trust him? Would the alcoholic husband have turned to drink if his wife's charity had encouraged his efforts to do his best, no matter what her personal ambitions might be? Would the irresponsible husband have jumped the reins if his wife's charity had considered him a loving partner in the give-and-take of marriage?

Our confessors may ponder, but the answers to these and similar questions must truthfully come from us. We may refuse to answer them in this life, but we shall be forced to answer them in eternity.

Marriage does not justify our imputing vices to our husbands, then complaining of the injuries done us. We cannot either in justice or in charity complain about our husband's faults without in some way making of ourselves a mirror reflecting the very faults we decry! Our husband and consequently our marriage will hardly be to our credit unless our charity helps them become so.

So, before charity can even begin to be effective in our home it must have a healthy beginning in our own soul. Unless charity is the strong and thriving virtue it should be we are endangering not only our own personal salvation, but also the sanctity and security of our marriage, and our relationship with our husband and our children.

In our relationship with our husband and children charity must be often practiced and applied. Charity needs to be put into practice as soon as Mrs. is prefixed to our name, and it needs to be constant from that moment on.

If marriage automatically, or magically fused two individuals into identical personalities with the same temperament and tastes; the same ideals and aspirations, charity would be easy to practice. However, despite the intimate relationship between the married partners, no such transformation takes place. The very intimacy of marriage rather tends to aggravate and exaggerate the personality contrasts of the two people involved. Although in marriage husband and wife become partners for life, they still remain distinct individuals. As children begin to evolve from the marriage, more individuals — each with its own distinct identity — round out the family.

Charity and charity alone recognizes and respects the inviolability of the individual's distinct identity; whether that individual be husband, children, or ourselves. Charity recognizes this inviolability because it understands the soul's personal and private relationship with God; a relationship which may never be invaded by another human being, no matter how intimate the human relationship may be. Charity also respects this inviolability because it acknowledges each soul as the temple of the Holy Spirit. Thus charity makes allowances for contrasts in personalities and causes love to thrive where otherwise friction would cause only discord and strife.

Within the circle of our marriage and among the assorted personalities of husband and children we can find all the opportunities we need to practice charity frequently, meritoriously, and even at times, heroically. Without even opening the door of our home, the constant application of charity in all the little things which make up our daily lives would make saints out of us!

THE FRUITS OF LOVE

Each virtue has its corresponding fruit. As we have seen, the predominant fruit of faith is peace, the predominant fruit of hope is joy, but the fruit of charity is the most delectable of all; an increase in love, a more intimate share in divine love.

Charity the most perfect virtue produces the most perfect fruit because the fruit of charity contains the mingling sweetness of all the fruits of all the virtues. Thus under the influence of divine love, the peace of faith becomes the serenity of love resting in the certitude of love; the joy of hope becomes the anticipation of consummated love awaiting in heaven, and charity becomes the union — even here — of the lover and the Beloved. Charity is the beginning of heaven upon earth.

But even more important perhaps, in the monotonous ticking off of our lives, charity truly lightens our burdens and makes the yoke of Christ sweet to bear. Under the influence of charity we develop the happy facility of perfectly keeping our house in order. Our housekeeping improves, both in the spiritual sense and in the temporal sense.

Since charity is the flame of divine love, it is necessarily a purifying flame. As it burns in our soul it destroys selfishness, the effects of sin, attachments to sin and all the dross which clutters up our soul and impedes the working of grace. As this spiritual trash pile dwindles and finally disappears, we find that the work of keeping our souls in order becomes amazingly simplified.

Our temporal housekeeping improves because charity has a way of improving not only our spiritual health but also our spiritual eyesight. Spiritual health improves because where there is charity there is no room for sloth and less room for the excuses which prevent us from doing what should be done when it should be done. Spiritual vision improves because charity strikes the scales of selfishness from our eyes allowing us to view everyone and everything in the true perspective of divine wisdom.

The life that may have seemed a hopeless tangle of loose ends seems almost magically to become a smoothly unwinding thread being woven somehow into God's mysteriously beautiful tapestry. Obligations and duties which make up the day of the wife and mother fall neatly into their proper places. There is enough time for everything, and all things are done well. The wisdom of charity teaches us that God gives us all the time we need to work out our salvation in the activity of love.

As charity increases in the soul it overflows and manifests itself in the spiritual and corporal works of mercy. All of the things we have been doing constantly for our family — sometimes passively, sometimes grudgingly, sometimes rebelliously — become, under the influence of charity, golden coins which we give back to God in exchange for a greater measure of His love.

God's love for us is infinite. For that reason we cannot even presume to say that the bond of love between the soul and God can be reciprocal in the same sense that it can be between two creatures. We may love God as perfectly as our humanity with its limitations would allow, but such a love would still fall so far short of God's love for us that it would be less than nothing. Divine love can be reciprocated only with divine love and it is precisely here that charity takes over and supplies what our limited human love lacks.

The supernatural virtue of charity in essence is the living flame of divine love which, when enkindled in the generous soul, bursts forth into the only love which can leap up and become one with divine love.

And so the day we awaken to the wonder that we are head over heels in love with God is a beautiful day indeed! On this day we may feel that we should venture out into the world to give a share of this new-found love to everyone we meet. We may even try! And in trying, discover something else: That God has been offering this same love to the world ever since it began, and the world is still not having any!

So in a way, Calvary begins for us with the dawn of love.

We would give Christ to others; instead we must go around taking a rejected Christ from them that He might have a resting place in our own heart. This inevitably is a soul-shaking experience, for with this experience comes sorrow; sorrow that we see others doing nothing more than we have done so many times before. And the tears of sorrow water the flowers of compassion, mercy, patience, and kindness.

With the blossoming of these flowers comes the understanding of another wonderful mystery: Christ loves those who have rejected Him just as much as He loves those who have sheltered Him! No longer do we feel any reservations concerning the second of charity's commandments: Love thy neighbor as thyself. Rather we feel the love which is Christ's love within us, go out from us to embrace all souls in the infinite circle of His arms.

And so this is charity: the soul's participation in the love which is God; love uncreated, personal, infinite. Love which, although infused into the soul by God, never becomes the soul's own. Rather, having its origin in God, even while burning in the soul, leaps always back into itself, to find itself and to be lost again within itself — God. This is the living flame of love, so intense and so all inclusive that it must reach out to include all souls within its warmth. Alive and active, this love cannot ever rest within itself or within ourselves, but must ever reach out to embrace and to be lost and found again within God and within all souls because they reflect His image and likeness.

And this also is charity: that we love God with our whole heart and soul and with all our strength — and our neighbor as ourself.

St. Paul tells us: "So there abide faith, hope and charity, these three; but the greatest of these is charity" (1 Cor. 13:13).

9

REFLECTIONS ON PURITY

*Jesus asks only that you sincerely give Him your heart; such is true
consecration. . . . Whatever difficulties may bring you today or
tomorrow you will no longer have those fears or sorrows that lead
to discouragement; because to be discouraged is to be disheartened,
and now you will have, instead of a weak human heart, a heart like
the Heart of God. Then you shall see verified in your family . . .
the Lord's promise to the Prophet Jeremias: "I will give them a
heart to know me . . . and they shall be my people, and I will be
their God; because they shall return to me with their whole
heart" (Jer. 24:7).*

THE CLEAN OF HEART

If you feel that you have lost your innocence because you are
married, you may have lost your innocence, but not because
you married. You lost your innocence in some other way.

The sacrament of matrimony was not instituted by Christ to
rob the married of their innocence; marriage was raised to a
sacrament by Christ to safeguard innocence. The sacramental
graces of our married state are intended to preserve our purity
and to keep it unspotted even while we share and enjoy our
conjugal love with our husband.

Perfect purity of conscience — cleanness of heart — is a prerogative which every wife and mother has a right to claim, to cherish, and to keep lustrous. If we happen to be among those who suspect that purity is lacking from our life it may be because we have an erroneous conception of the meaning of purity in its broad sense; or that we are not living in the state of grace; or because chastity is not being practiced as perfectly as it should be.

There seems to be a trend of thinking among the married that purity and chastity are the same "virtue," and that marriage is its negation. Actually, purity and chastity are not the same; there is a definite difference between them. Purity, which is the luminous innocence of the clean of heart is a state — more precisely a state of grace in which the soul enjoys freedom from all sin. Chastity is a virtue; a power to act in a supernatural way to avoid the sins of lust. Neither purity nor chastity are violated from the pleasure inherent in the conjugal act unless that pleasure is a sinful perversion of its divine purpose — procreation.

And yet, there are those who define evil as a three-letter word spelled s-e-x! To such, childhood is purity; youthful virginity is purity; and adult virginity, besides being purity, is also the essence of virtue. Such thinking usually goes further to surmise that original sin was committed the instant Adam and Eve discovered mutual delight in their conjugal love; that sex is an illicit pleasure enjoyed by the promiscuous, and shunned (or at least not admitted) by the virtuous — even in marriage. And so, the conclusion drawn is that although marriage may be respectability, it is not the fertile field of sanctity; and the day that virginity is exchanged for maternity, innocence, chastity, and consequent purity are ravished and put to death, never more to be claimed even by the good Catholic wife and mother. And this state of mind could very easily discourage us both from aspiring to perfect our own purity, and from ever reaching the degree of sanctity willed for us by God Himself.

Physical childhood in itself is not the essence of purity even though children lack experimental knowledge of serious sin. We know how persistently our own children have to be guided toward virtue, for by reason of original sin children are inclined to sinfulness, even as we are. Sin can be as fascinating to children as it can be to any one of us, and we should never complacently rely upon their tender years to keep them unspotted.

The evidence of original sin's hold upon our children may be observed in their predisposition to disobedience, selfishness, cruelty, untruthfulness, dishonesty, anger, greediness. We need only to remember our own childhood to realize the truth of our awakening to sin almost simultaneously with our awakening to reason. We need only to observe our own children's selfish tantrums, disobedience, and clamorings for attention to have this truth verified. Our children's natural tendencies — most of them — are tainted with impurity and these natural tendencies usually have nothing at all to do with sexual knowledge or experience.

Neither is virginity, whether youthful or mature, necessarily purity in a strict sense; nor is it always the essence of virtue, nor the perfection of the virtue of chastity. Actually virginity is not even virtuous if it is merely the consequence of circumstance; that is, virginity retained because of the inability to find a suitable spouse. Thus the mere physical integrity which we call virginity does not assure a higher degree of purity than virginity exchanged for the privilege of maternity.

Only virginity which is consecrated, which offers itself as a pure gift to God, sealed and untampered, diffuses the sweet essence of purity and becomes at the same time the perfection of the virtue of chastity as it is practiced by priests and religious or by lay persons who have foregone the legitimate pleasure of sex in order to serve God more freely and more perfectly.

The transition from virginity to maternity which all mothers make should not affect our purity at all; except to increase and to perfect it. As wives and mothers we are privileged to delight in our conjugal love; we are privileged to enjoy maternal love and through both of these loves we are predisposed to grow in perfect purity of conscience which should help us also to grow in perfect love of God and live in intimate union with Him.

INNOCENCE IS NOT IGNORANCE

Purity is not the innocence which merely connotes lack of sexual knowledge and experience. Perfect purity of conscience is the innocence which is *free* from sin. And here again we run into a trend of erroneous thinking. Despite the fact that our Faith definitely classifies different kinds of sin, there is a common misconception that the sexual urge is the main cause of serious sin.

If we find that any reference to serious sin immediately causes us to associate the word *sin* with some aspect of sex, we had better begin a revision of our understanding of sin. In the first place, there is nothing evil about sex nor the pleasure inherent in the sexual act as it is given to humanity from the hand of God. Yet despite the frequent emphasis placed upon this truth we keep insisting upon surrounding something which is sacred and holy with an aura of impurity. In the second place, sex becomes sinful only from our abuse of it or from the perversion caused by our sinful inclinations which would degenerate a sublime loving act into a lustful pleasure. Furthermore, in addition to lust (*not* sex) there are six other capital sins, each more deadly than the other.

Perfect purity of heart would presuppose freedom, not only from the sin of lust but from all serious sin; for purity in its broad sense has only as much to do with the absence of lust in our lives as it has to do with the absence of pride, covetousness, gluttony, anger, sloth, envy. We cannot be pure if we nourish six of the capital sins in our soul and avoid the seventh, any more than we can claim purity in being lustful while scrupulously avoiding all the other capital sins.

And yet purity is more than refraining from the actual commission of sin. It presupposes also a complete freedom from all voluntary attachments to sin. For example, if we pride ourselves in the fact that we do not ever commit serious sin, that is, perform the sinful act, yet allow our desires and thoughts licentious freedom to play with the fascination of sin we are not only guilty of self-deception, but also of allowing our souls to be contaminated by the grossest impurity.

This, in a sense, would be like priding ourselves in never missing Mass on Sunday while habitually robbing a bank on Monday; or like miserly living in poverty while our greed gorges itself upon a hidden hoard of gold. Neither the thief who always hears Mass nor the miser who practices poverty can be called virtuous by any standard except self-deception. And neither can we be numbered among the clean of heart unless we relinquish, not only the act of sinning, but also all attachments to sin.

By the same token, we cannot enhance our own reputation by stealing our neighbor's good name by calumny or detraction. We cannot point to our marriage as the perfect acceptance of God's will if we envy Mrs. So and So's new fur coat while resentment murders our appreciation for this year's new baby; nor can we profitably refrain from overindulgence in food or drink if we allow our souls to grow fat with malice from feeding our mind with inordinate curiosity; nor can we complacently claim avoidance of sloth by being meticulous housekeepers if we relegate our spiritual exercises to a kind of sleepy ennui. And so on.

Any one of these clandestine attachments to the capital sins can be serious, or not so serious, depending upon how frequently and how inordinately they are indulged. But any one of them, serious or not, is incompatible with the perfection of purity. Any one of them darkens our soul and keeps it from enjoying the perfect purity of conscience which must be ours in order to become "like little children" (Mt. 18:3).

Although purity of conscience may be defined as the soul's freedom and detachment from sin, perfect purity of conscience is not necessarily dependent upon our lack of knowledge or experience of sin. Innocence is perfected in wisdom, not in ignorance. We come to know and understand sin in proportion to our nearness to God and the consequent purity of our conscience. We never come to know and understand sin through the familiarity of commission. In committing sin, either habitually or intermittently, we shut our divine light in our soul and lose the ability to see clearly by the light of truth. Once this light dims or is gone, we tend more or less to grope blindly from the impetus of self-love. Self-love knows nothing of truth for it stays too preoccupied trying to make virtue out of vice.

In examining the lives of the saints we find that they entered the realm of spiritual childhood by an infinite number of paths. Some arrived by traveling first the broad highway of sin; others never deviated from the narrow path which took them in their baptismal innocence straight to God. All of them, though, enjoyed intimate union with God in perfect purity of conscience because they knew sin for what it is and despised and avoided it accordingly.

Even those saints who were granted the privilege of seeing souls in the state of mortal sin lost none of their purity in thus looking upon sin, even though such a vision might bring to light all the hidden aspects of sin; many of which sinners are usually unaware. On the contrary, they were cognizant at once of the vileness of sin and of the weakness of the sinner. They shared God's viewpoint concerning sin; and because it was God's viewpoint their innocence and purity were confirmed and strengthened, their love for God was intensified and their passion for the salvation of sinners was inflamed, while at the same time their compassion for sinners was deepened.

THE FLAWLESS CRYSTAL OF PURITY

Purity of conscience, cleanness of heart, is the most precious adornment the soul can possess. It is like a sparkling jewel, so pleasing to God because it reflects His own divine purity and places us in His sight again as a little child clothed in baptismal innocence.

Such purity must be ours if we would desire an intimate relationship with God; such purity can be ours if we work for its perfection. In so working we should never lose sight of the fact that the excellence of the finished jewel is dependent upon two things: our own sincere efforts and the efficacious help of God's grace. We cannot presume to perfect purity in our souls without God's help; nor will God perfect purity in us without our co-operation.

The flawless crystal of purity then becomes cut and polished by the rooting out of our bad habits and our attachments to them. We must work constantly also to rid our soul of all harmful attachments to persons, places, and things; we must conscientiously avoid all occasions of sin; we must strive always to know, love, and serve God as perfectly as we can in whatever our state in life demands of us. And we must cultivate virtue. Not by merely wishing to be virtuous, but by the active practice of all the virtues.

While examining the crystal of purity it would be well to take note of another facet of the same gem: purity of intention. We cannot attain perfect purity of conscience if our intentions need to be purified, any more than we could claim to have a clean home if our floors need to be scrubbed. And here again the term "intentions that are not pure," does not mean the intention of committing adultery at the first opportunity, nor even the intention of telling off-color jokes at the next social gathering. Purity of intention simply means doing all things for the love of God; doing all things in response to God's will for us in the present moment, and doing all things with disregard for self.

It is easy for us to do anything, no matter how disagreeable a task might be in itself, so long as we are able to rest in the appreciation of what we have done. However, it is usually seldom rather than frequently that we are privileged to bask in the warmth of loving appreciation from any of those to whom we render service. Because of this apparent lack of appreciation, our disagreeable tasks become not only more disagreeable, they become downright soul-searing grievances which could propel us into neurosis — if not into insanity. Thank God they can also propel us into sanctity.

If we are aiming for sanctity, purity of intention becomes the bridge over which we bypass the annoyance inherent in tedious monotony: service unappreciated, self-sacrifice taken for granted; and by which we stay above the impure involvement in a task for self-satisfaction and find joy and peace in the performance of a task for the love of God. A task thus performed is done well, cheerfully and without undue reflection. That is, it is not held in the mind in order to feed our self-pity, or to aggravate our annoyance or resentment. Once done it is relegated to God and forgotten by us. And being forgotten, the stress of annoyance over any lack of appreciation is removed. If we are appreciated, we are pleasantly surprised, if not, we are unconcerned for our joy in working for the love of God is not dependent upon appreciation — from our families nor anyone else.

The degree of purity with which our intentions are permeated has much to do with the sanctification of ourself in the doing of all things in response to God's will for us in the present moment. As our intentions become more pure we become more and more conscious of what is expected of us here and now. We learn to concentrate our spiritual energy toward God and what He has given us to do in the present moment. We leave the past and the future where they belong, in His hands.

No longer do we try to steal God's prerogative of seeing and knowing all things at once. No longer do we try to gather fruit before we have planted the seed. No longer does our reflection of the past and our anticipation of the future crowd our present with regret, apprehension, and impatience. Rather we remain lightly poised in the present, keeping our hands upon our work and our eyes upon God. The past falls behind us and the future becomes nothing more than the manifestation of God's will for us here and now. Whatever plans we may have had for our future, center now in God. Our living becomes simplified because we live simply in God.

Purity, besides being innocence and cleanness of heart, is the flawless crystal in which we find and recognize our resemblance to God. Holding in its heart the essence of all virtue, purity distills from its depths the perfume of sanctity. The crystal keeps unimpaired within its center the vision which is granted the children to whom our Lord was referring when He said: "Blessed are the pure of heart, for they shall see God" (Mt. 5:8). Purity clears the eyes of the soul and gives us this vision of God; darkly in this life, face to face in heaven.

And so in order to enjoy the face to face vision of God in heaven, our soul must be adorned with the purity which is the reflection of God's perfect purity. At the moment of death, our soul will leap up and be lost in the flame of divine love; or it will shrivel and burn in the dark vacuum of self-love, depending upon the purity we possess — or lack — when God calls us to be judged.

If we save our impurity for purgatory it will go along with us to be the cause of our soul's suffering until every vestige of it is burned away. If we tenaciously cling to impurity that we might enjoy it for eternity, we shall take it to hell where impurity will prod us forever with unspeakable torment.

On the other hand, if we prepare for our death by cultivating the atmosphere of purity in our lives by prayer, mortification, and the active practice of all the virtues — in short if we "become again like little children" our death will be the opening of God's arms that we may be lost in His embrace for all eternity.

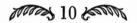

10

REFLECTIONS ON CONJUGAL CHASTITY

By virtue of the Sacrament of Matrimony a human institution — the family community is transformed into an instrument of divine action . . . it is directly sanctified and your conjugal union itself receives a very particular imprint of God . . . it is necessary that there be born in you, and always grow stronger, the determined will to be holy . . . in your conjugal union itself and in the very exercise of your love (Pius XII, July 13, 1958).

CHASTITY THE VIRTUE

Besides the theological virtues which regulate our relationship with God, we have the moral virtues which regulate our personal and social behavior. There are four of these virtues: prudence, temperance, fortitude, and justice.

Temperance is the virtue which provides the supernatural help we need to keep well ordered our appetites or desires for the pleasures of sense. Chastity is part of this virtue for it is chastity which regulates the right use of the sexual appetite.

For some reason there seems to be a misconception among the married that chastity is not an integral part of marriage. This misconception probably has root in the fact that religious take a vow of chastity and by that vow relinquish the privilege of marrying, while the married by reason of their marriage vows have the privilege of exercising the generative faculty.

In other words, chastity and the fulfillment of the marital obligation have become disassociated; the idea being that celibates and virgins practice the virtue of chastity and married people do not. This is a mistaken understanding of the virtue for the practice of chastity is just as important for the married as it is for the religious or unmarried. And the practice of chastity for the married is not confined to the times of voluntary continence, as some believe; but to every aspect of the conjugal relationship between husband and wife.

If chastity is not for the married, why then would the Church pray ". . . true and chaste may she marry in Christ, and be a follower of holy women . . . may she be fruitful in offspring. May her life be pure and blameless . . ." (Prayer from the Nuptial Mass). In this prayer we have every proof we need that marriage is to be a safeguard for chastity for us, not a violation of it!

Chastity then for us who are married is simply this: a holy reverence for the sacred function of sex. If this holy reverence is cultivated and cherished; if the marital act stays surrounded by this atmosphere of holy reverence, then our marriage is not only chaste, but the virtue of chastity is being practiced as it should be in our state in life.

The joys and delights of marriage are at the same time channels of grace. This would seem almost too wonderful to be true! But it is true; and because it is true, we pause to wonder why all of us who are married do not automatically become saints.

There are many reasons why we do not, but one of the fundamental reasons is that the pleasure inherent in the physical expression of conjugal love is rooted in the animal nature which exerts a tendency to pull us, by way of the sense appetites, away from the supernatural plane in which our souls would dwell.

In marriage there is always the danger that we may become so enthralled with the enjoyment of a legitimate pleasure that we set it up as a false idol; worshiping it as the sole end of marriage, or worse yet, as the sole end of existence. If this happens, chastity is violated and lust takes over. Once this happens, no longer is the sexual function considered a pure gift from God, but rather it is snatched from His hands and claimed as a just due — a pleasure to use and even abuse if necessary just so enjoyment is not disturbed nor interrupted. Serious sin results because the beauty of chastity loses its appeal. The tendency, then, is to wallow in the mud of animal passion, desiring only to be satisfied.

Sexual indulgence in marriage, separated from chastity, is sinful; and sinful sexual indulgence in marriage is the cause of most of the social evils about which we complain. Divorce, birth control, illegal abortion, juvenile delinquency; nearly every isolated case of any one of these social evils has its roots in the perversion of the sacred purpose of marriage. Chastity violated beneath the cloak of marriage wreaks terrible vengeance — on individual marriages, on society!

That our lives are a continual battle of the flesh against the spirit is one of the most fundamental lessons we have to learn. It is worse than foolish to presume that such a battle is not for the married. It is no more than prudent to be prepared for this warfare by wearing the armor of chastity.

CHASTITY AND INHIBITIONS

As women, we usually sense the spiritual dangers in marriage for our feminine sense of delicacy is normally attracted to that which is clean, pure, and wholesome. As Catholic wives we should beware, though, that our sense of delicacy does not foster inhibitions which would falsely accuse us of violating chastity.

There are many reasons why we either enter marriage with inhibitions or find them growing worse as the years of marriage go on. Fundamentally inhibitions are usually the result of ignorance. And here again ignorance is not to be confused with innocence! Innocence, in this case the lack of sexual experience, should be the perfect wedding gift given to a spouse; ignorance should not be allowed to ruin the mutual enjoyment of that gift.

Precise instructions on all the points of the physical aspects of marriage relations should be a premarital must! Most parishes provide such instructions and recommend supplementary reading. Both engaged couples and the married who might be floundering in inhibited spiritual insecurity should avail themselves of such instructions.

It cannot be insisted too emphatically that such instruction be gotten from a reliable source. And a reliable source is not necessarily a mother, an aunt, nor even an intimate friend. Too many women, youthful or mature, have neither the certitude of what constitutes normal virtue in marriage nor the ability to discuss in detail, which proves more often than not a source of embarrassment. Most women shy away from discussing sexual intimacies, and even if questioned veil their answers with implications which may leave one even more inhibited than before.

For example there are not too many women who will frankly admit that they enjoy their marital relations. For some reason there seems to be an unspoken law which forbids such an admission on the grounds that it would brand them as promiscuous. In fact there are some women who, although the mothers of good size families, emphatically insist that they have never, in all their married lives, ever "given in" to sexual pleasure. The implication being that they are thereby more virtuous than the common run-of-the-mill wife who might happen to enjoy her husband's love-making!

Pity the poor daughter of such a mother, if her inherited attitude toward sex is shocked by the discovery after marriage that sexual intercourse is enjoyable! Unless enlightened to the contrary, she may go through her whole married life suffering from a false conscience resulting from inhibitions which confuse the pleasure of sex with sin. She may never sin in the slightest degree against chastity yet, at the same time never ever rid herself of the certitude that the pleasure of sex taints her with impurity.

To such wives confession after marriage can become a torment for they can never be quite sure whether they have sinned or not. Their confessors never succeed in completely reassuring them, for discussing such a subject in confession fills them with embarrassment and confusion.

Inhibitions in themselves are not sins, but they can be a favorite playground for the devil. Although he does not have the power to cause us to commit sin through them, he can exaggerate them in our minds to the extent that they impede our spiritual progress. The devil usually takes advantage of our inhibitions to tempt us against hope; the hope that we can ever be pure in our marriage, the hopelessness of receiving Holy Communion frequently in the impure state over which we apparently have no control, the hopelessness of striving for perfection since perfection cannot be realized without chastity. The devil works overtime trying to convince the married that chastity is no longer theirs to claim!

Herein lies the real spiritual danger of inhibitions: they work persistently to smother the soul's supernatural tendency to seek God as the first cause and last end of marriage. An inhibited soul can never attain union with God unless it first gets rid of its inhibitions; and this it can only do by approaching them intelligently, by seeking the truth about conjugal love and putting the knowledge gained into practice. Inhibitions in the newly married are understandable; in those who have been married any length of time they are inexcusable. Inhibitions not only make us miserable, they cause our own misery to infect the soul of our marriage, robbing ourselves and our spouse of its satisfying conjugal fruits.

VIOLATIONS OF CONJUGAL CHASTITY

One of the most serious sins against chastity in marriage is adultery, and there are two common aspects of this sin. One is that sin which still shocks and scandalizes most respectable people; the sexual involvement of a married person with some-one other than the married partner. The other is that form of adultery which has become so socially acceptable as to cause hardly a raised eyebrow even among so-called good Catholics: the adulterous practice of marrying divorced persons.

The first is usually avoided at least for self-respect if for no other reason, but divorce and remarriage in this day and age is something else again. It is another good example of what can happen because of the disassociation of ideas. Popular opinion notwithstanding, adultery is adultery. Divorce and remarriage may legalize it and cover it with the cloak of respectability but no one has found a way yet of sanctifying such a practice in God's eyes!

Considering the frequency with which the sixth commandment is broken in this regard, it should follow that those of us Catholic mothers who are interested in the sanctity of marriage should wonder just where the blame lies.

With society? Society never has particularly contributed to the advancement of virtue, and in this generation seems to be working overtime at glorifying vice and trying to impose it upon the individual. Society could be blamed for the appalling viola-tions against conjugal chastity except for one fact — we as in-dividuals make up the very society we deplore!

Can the blame be placed upon those who enter adulterous marriages simply because they should know better than to choose willfully the way of the flesh instead of the spirit? We cannot discount their culpability entirely, but why have they fallen into such callous disregard for virtue and the sanctity of marriage? We could keep asking "why?" all the rest of our lives, then ignore the answer because the answer is found too close to home. We close our eyes and ears and hearts against the truth because truth would insist that most of the blame lies with us!

We may vehemently deny that the blame comes anywhere near us; insisting that the blame must lie with society rather than with ourselves or with our children. How we love to generalize! But if we would be truthful with ourselves we must stop dealing in generalities and get down to particulars.

And the particulars are these: Is society winning the war which we are too weak or too cowardly to fight? Have we lost so completely our sense of eternal values that we no longer recognize sin as the evil it is? Has our Faith lost the vigor it needs to counteract the salacious conditioning to which we have become exposed through the glorification of lust as it is presented on all sides? In preparing our children to take their places as respectable members of society have we neglected to teach them the difference between respectability and virtue? Have we neglected to impress our children with the fact that members of society are also members of the Mystical Body of Christ?

It is tragic indeed that too many of us Catholic mothers have to check off most or even all of these answers in the affirmative.

And we watch our children's involvement with those they cannot validly marry, yet close our eyes against the almost inevitable outcome. Our Johnnys and Marys are merely enjoying harmless companionships (we tell ourselves). Nothing can possibly come of it. And when the inevitable happens, we go into hysterics, then kiss the bride and groom (we cannot do anything else about it anyway), wish them happiness and point with pride forever after to the successful marriage of those two!

How can we call ourselves good Catholic wives and mothers, yet condone the sin of adultery in our children? Yet we do! Any parish priest will testify to the fact that except for the first distraught reaction to the shock, it is all too seldom that a mother will consider her child's invalid marriage as anything else than an innocent involvement in an unfortunate circumstance; and some do not even consider it an unfortunate circumstance if the marriage is materially successful.

There was a time when even society ostracized those who divorced and dared remarry. Society has legalized such a practice; the Church has not. If we have allowed our convictions to be weakened to the point where we have lost the true perspective of such marriages, then we are providing society with another weapon to use against us. We and our children become living proof that invalid marriages cannot be nearly so bad as our religion would make them. We in turn add to the social evils we complain about!

How many of us, too, are responsible for our children's spiritual death because in neglecting our own spiritual education we have neglected to provide positive instruction in virtue along with their other education. If we are bound to educate our children that they may someday contribute to the welfare of society, as Catholics we are even more strictly obligated to prepare our children to become healthy members of the Mystical Body of Christ. Our moral obligation toward our children, then, is not only to give them good example but to instruct them in virtue and to encourage them in the active practice of the virtues.

And chastity takes its place among the most important of the virtues. Upon the high regard for chastity which is planted in the child's soul depend the youth's and the adult's habitual practice of this virtue and the insurance against the adulterous alliance of an invalid marriage.

Almost from infancy a child needs to be instructed and gently encouraged in the practice of chastity. And the day upon which the study of the Ten Commandments begins is not too early to begin the conditioning against invalid marriage. The Sixth Commandment will inevitably pose the question, "what is adultery?" and with our answer begins our child's indoctrination.

Let us never stand accused before our children by answering this particular question with a vague reference to impurity, with implications slanted toward dirty thoughts, dirty jokes, and actions which are "not nice." Of course the Sixth Commandment will offer opportunity to instruct along these lines also, but these things are not adultery strictly speaking. In explaining adultery we should be truthful, otherwise the child's curiosity will be aroused rather than satisfied.

In answering this question, we need only to associate adultery with divorce in the child's mind. We need only explain that if a man and wife divorce each other and marry someone else, the resulting sin is adultery; and to emphasize further that such a sin is so serious that whoever commits it may never receive Holy Communion again while living in that sin.

As our children mature we should always encourage spontaneous family discussion of the virtues in general and of chastity in particular; emphasizing always the sacredness of the human body; the sacredness of marriage as the guardian of the family's spiritual and temporal welfare, and as the only state in life in which sex can be used according to God's plan, and so on.

And never should we minimize the Church's stand against invalid marriage. For the Church there is no justifiable reason for it; from our standpoint there can be no justifiable reason either.

Another serious sin against chastity in marriage is artificial birth control. Whether or not we have allowed our awareness of this sin to be dulled by the forceful arguments put forth by society in general and the proponents of planned parenthood in particular, the fact remains that it is a serious sin.

Along with adultery it is the worst violation of the virtue of chastity that married people commit. It matters little whether conception is avoided by the use of contraceptives — either mechanical or chemical — or by the variety of other means that might be used to precipitate sexual satisfaction. What matters is that any voluntary perversion of the marital act defeats the primary purpose of marriage and so is mortally sinful. Such sins are as detestable in the sight of God today as they were the day God struck Onan dead because he had spilled his seed upon the ground (cf. Gen. 38:8–10).

We have absolutely no right to tamper with sex and pervert its end toward our own lustful satisfaction; nor does marriage give us the right to do so. Marriage gives us the right only to the legitimate use of sex as God's plan for us: that we become procreators with Him that other human beings may come into the world from His hands through us, if God so wills it. This is the primary purpose of marriage; its secondary purpose is the expression of conjugal love, which expression is realized fully and completely only in the mutual and pure enjoyment of the marriage act by husband and wife.

And so because God has seen fit to make this expression of conjugal love so strong and so deep, we fret and even transgress in our rebellion against the God-given law which also encompasses it.

With the birth of our first child our conjugal love retreats into a kind of dark room of fear haunted by one specter: pregnancy! In our weakness we come to despise the sexual urge and repress it; or we give in to the temptation to express it sinfully then try to draw comfort from the fact that our marriage has all the outward marks of respectability.

Respectability! How many of us fall into the vicious habit of trading the sacramental graces of marriage for their counterfeit, respectability — the devil's contribution to the welfare of society!

Substituting respectability for virtue in marriage is the same as walking down the steps to hell! And yet, respectability has become so subtly and so firmly seated in virtue's place that it would try to convince us now that children are the abuse, rather than the fruit of conjugal love. Large families are blamed for every evil existing today from the blighting of neighborhoods to the undermining of social morality.

Our courage is hardly a shield against the attacks of those who raise their eyebrows because our maternity wardrobe serves more than one season's wear. Those who argue that sexual gratification is an integral part of our physical welfare, at the same time concern themselves with the shocking lack of "self-control" of those who would fill their homes with children. Society judges us respectable or promiscuous, by counting our children's noses. And the temptation to resort to the use of contraceptives becomes, in our minds, not so much sinful as expedient; for we would maintain respectability even at the cost of virtue.

If, in this respectable state, we do not fall away from our Catholic Faith altogether, we are likely to spend the rest of our child-bearing years hunting for the one priest in the Catholic Church who will respect our respectability and understand all the "grave reasons" why we be allowed to continue in this way of life. That we never obtain such permission is a tribute to our priests and to the paternal interest they have for the welfare of our souls. No priest in the hierarchy of the Catholic Church — including the pope — could ever give anyone permission to practice artificial birth control for any reason, however grave or expedient. In so doing our spiritual fathers would be condoning the mortal sins of their spiritual children and encouraging our willful determination to use our marriage license as a one-way ticket to hell. They would be betraying their sacred trust becoming, in the words of Christ, "blind and leaders of the blind: and if the blind lead the blind, both fall into the pit" (Mt. 15:14).

To presume that chastity might be regained, or even annexed to respectability, after the possibility of pregnancy is no more, is a dangerous spiritual gamble. The danger is not that God will desert us, for His grace never ceases to flow in our direction as long as we live; the danger is in our own smug, self-sufficient respectability. When the end of our life comes, we are not likely to want to destroy the wall that has (we hope) hidden us from God. After all, that wall of separation took a lifetime to build! Its shade and protection have become comforting to the weak, blind eyes of our soul. The tragedy is that we may prefer to die on the side of its darkness, for it has become the only comfort we know!

That it is not God's will that anyone die in such a miserable state is evinced over and over. No matter how self-complacent a person is, or has been in sin, it is inevitable that a time must come when that soul must become overwhelmed with the sickening impurity of such a marriage. And society has yet to come up with a brand of soap which will wash this particular stench away! That God steps in with a sudden enlightenment as to the state of such a soul is a definite sign that He would have another marriage conformed to His plan. In God's sight, it matters not at all what the past has been; what matters is the co-operation given to the grace He offers now.

For He would show His children even now, even after they have offended Him so much, that He loves them, is mindful of them, and will help them if they accept the love and the help He offers. There is no need to linger in any false conviction that chastity once ravished cannot be regained. It can be. Naturally, there will be a struggle involved, but with God's help and a determined will it may be claimed again as the bright star of marriage. Furthermore, with the help of God's grace, as each temptation against chastity is met and vanquished, one may go on persevering in the perfection of chastity until the end of life.

THE HIDDEN VIOLATIONS

Besides the glaring sins against chastity in marriage, adultery and artificial birth control, there are what we might call less obvious sins. They are less obvious because they are rarely admitted and even less rarely mentioned. Yet despite the fact that these sins keep themselves so well hidden they can be, nevertheless, serious transgressions against chastity. These sins have their beginnings in our licentious mental associations with the legitimate marital act.

Since the pleasure inherent in sex has its roots in the animal nature it is not unusual for us to be tempted to sin mentally, even while avoiding any physical act of sinning.

For example: inadvertently, it may be discovered that the pleasure of the marital act is incited to a greater intensity from the stimulus of obscene thoughts or imaginings. Since this new discovery may be an enjoyable sensation, such thoughts or imaginings may be deliberately recalled in order to recapture such enjoyment.

This mental transgression against chastity is not so likely to occur during the early years of marriage, for then the whole enjoyment of the conjugal act is centered in the new spouse and the newness of this delight is enough to fan the flame of natural desire. But settled in the everyday sameness of married life, there may be the inclination to become bored with what seems to have become a routine ritual. The physical expression of love becomes monotonous and desire responds very, very reluctantly. If the tendency is toward scrupulousness, there may be the fear that failure to respond to a spouse's demands may be a failing in conjugal obligation. Impure mental gymnastics become a means of supplying the excitement which monotony fails to arouse.

Stimulating desire from lustful thoughts is fatal to virtue. Such a habit will inevitably weaken the virtue of chastity, and the pure seal of marriage will be broken.

Conscience will be the first to protest such a vile habit; yet we may, in avoiding the actual commission of sin, try to rest in the conviction that we are becoming inhibited. If we persist in such a habit, we shall have to admit one day that chastity is no longer ours to claim as a safeguard for the sanctity of our marriage. It inevitably happens that continence must be practiced at times in every marriage. When these times occur for us, we are in danger then of resorting to sinful practices to supply the pleasure that lustful desires may then demand. Chastity, having been violated, will be no longer present to sustain us.

In the same way we can mentally commit adultery; even though we may pride ourselves in the fact that we have never ever indulged in sexual experience outside of our marriage. However, the reading of too many romantic novels, seeing too many movies, watching too many TV shows, can be the occasions precipitating us into this kind of mental sin. All we need to do to make this sin serious is willfully invite some imagined lover to take the place of our spouse in our mind and then enjoy the consequent imaginary, forbidden pleasure.

There is almost an infinite variety of lustful stimuli always at the disposal of the married. The basic trouble with most of us is that we furtively nibble at this forbidden fruit and then refuse to admit our contamination from it. We allow such transgressions to make an insidious inroad into our marriage, then hide behind the generalization that chastity and the married state are incompatible.

Generalizations notwithstanding, we must someday account for the chastity of our marriage. It is God's will that marriage and chastity be compatible. It is our spiritual obligation to be certain that they are.

CHASTITY AND RHYTHM

Periodic abstinence from marriage relations, or rhythm, although not a deliberate frustration of the natural purpose of the conjugal act, does not always add to the sanctity and happiness of marriage. As a matter of fact there are some circumstances which make the practice of rhythm sinful. And so, before we commend ourselves too highly on our virtuous self-control we should pause to realize that such self-control is merely allowed if there are justifiable reasons; and whether these justifiable reasons are temporary or without time limit.

For example, there are certain circumstances which would justify the use of the safe period only temporarily and among these would be: the temporary weakness or illness of the mother; after a recent pregnancy; because of frequent pregnancies too close together; temporary economic difficulties and for the establishing of mutual agreement between partners who may agree over intercourse but not over a new pregnancy in the near future.

Only more serious circumstances justify the use of the safe period without time limit and among these are: a grave endangering of the wife's health from pregnancy; the likelihood of children being stillborn or defective; reasonable fear of miscarriage; incurable, hereditary disease; grave economic difficulties resulting from an addition to the family.

Although most of us have a fairly good idea of the circumstances which govern our lives, we do not have the privilege of letting a false sense of values color these circumstances. So before we whimsically resort to the practice of rhythm for whatever reason, and however justifiable it may seem to us, we should take the problem to our confessor for advice and guidance.

We should ponder, too, the words of Pope Pius XII as he warns those who would resort to the use of rhythm as a means of escaping the responsibilities of marriage:

"If, however, in the light of a reasonable and fair judgment, there are no such serious personal reasons, or reasons deriving from external personal reasons, or reasons deriving from external circumstances, then the habitual intention to avoid the fruitfulness of the union, while at the same time continuing fully to satisfy sensual intent, can only arise from a false appreciation of life and from motives that run counter to true standards of moral conduct" (Discourse to Members of the Congress of the Italian Association of Catholic Midwives, October 9, 1951).

And so our marriage cannot be conformed to God's plan if rhythm is whimsically used solely to foster the material success of our marriage. We cannot truthfully call our marriage virtuous if we deliberately time our love-making with the intentions of combining a fruitless marriage with a successful career. Although it is true that such a discreet way of avoiding pregnancy does not frustrate the natural end of the conjugal act, it is just as true that it can frustrate the primary end of marriage — raising a family.

The transgression here is against charity rather than against chastity. We cannot profess to love God if we continually refuse to conform our marriage to His divine will. Perfect charity, since it must be devoid of selfishness, demands that our conjugal love be a means of co-operating with God's creative plan as well as a means of expressing conjugal love by physical union. If the intentions motivating the practice of rhythm are primarily selfish, having as their sole end the avoidance of pregnancy, it naturally follows that we may also tend to seek and obtain this end by an uncharitable disregard for our spouse's spiritual well-being.

Lacking mutual consent, the imposition of abstinence by one spouse upon another is also a sin against justice. Justice is violated because the very contract of marriage is violated. Since the marriage contract is an agreement whereby those married freely yield to and accept from each other the exclusive right to the marriage act, neither married partner has the right to impose continence upon the other against his or her reasonable wishes. This can be a grave injustice if one partner's wishes happen to be conformed to God's will in regard to accepting any children He may choose to send.

Wives, especially, often deserve a reprimand for this transgression although we hear of husbands who are so solicitous for the things of the world that they refuse their wives nothing — except the privilege of motherhood.

Paradoxically, rhythm can be a potential threat to the virtue of chastity, especially to the chastity of the spouse upon whom continence is imposed. If, within marriage, the legitimate satisfaction of the concupiscent appetite is denied a partner, he or she may fall prey to the temptations to commit adultery or any of the various other sins against chastity. Here again, if the practice of rhythm is motivated solely by a selfish desire to avoid pregnancy, our presumably virtuous abstinence may turn against us and become no more than an excuse either to resort to the use of contraceptives, or to the unprotested consent of their use.

Finally, a deliberately prolonged avoidance of pregnancy, even by voluntary continence, shows our lack of faith in God and trust in His divine Providence. Christ has emphatically told us who have such little faith: "But seek first the kingdom of God and His justice, and all these things shall be given you besides" (Mt. 6:34).

God proves His loving paternal care for us over and over when even the most grave reasons for avoiding pregnancy miraculously improve for those who offer their conjugal love as a pure unselfish gift to Him as proof of their love for Him and trust in Him.

CHASTITY AND CONTINENCE

The total continence which most "spiritual" people presumably practice — as though continence were the only requirement upon which holiness hinges — is more a false premise than an actuality. As a matter of fact, we may not impose continence upon a married partner for spiritual reasons any more than we may impose it for any other reason previously mentioned. Here again there must be mutual consent, which in turn should be submitted to the advice and guidance of a confessor. The truth, though, is that this mutual consent more often than not is never reached because one of the married partners usually is convinced that total continence — even for the love of God — is carrying spirituality too far!

Which brings up the question: if one married partner desires to live in total continence for the love of God, and the other refuses, does this cause unhappiness in marriage?

It can, but it should not.

If we have reached a degree of holiness which inflames our desire to live in complete abstinence; we must necessarily have the degree of sanity which admits that the impossibility of realizing this desire is not detrimental to our perfection. If this desire takes precedence over our spouse's wishes and fills us with self-righteous opinions as to who is pure and who is not pure in our marriage, then we are living in the false spirituality of self-love.

True holiness tolerates nothing selfish, not even desires that are apparently holy. True sanctity submits even our holy desires to God's will to be fulfilled or not as He sees fit. So if it is not God's will that we walk toward Him in continence, we continue walking toward Him by joyfully fulfilling the conjugal obligations which marriage imposes upon us.

To presume that only those married persons who practice total continence have a claim to sanctity is heresy. It is the presumption that God who is all good, and who can never err, slipped up on the means ordained by Him to propagate the human race; that those who legitimately use the gift He ordained for that purpose are excluded from the company of saints unless they forego the use of the very means He ordained for the propagation of the human race. This kind of circuitous thinking can never be conducive to sanctity for it does not even admit of common sense!

That God depends upon chaste conjugal love to carry out His plans for us has been proved countless times, beginning with His command that Adam and Eve increase and multiply, down to the present day. There is not a saint in heaven whose state of being was not dependent upon the mutual co-operation between conjugal love and divine love. If that one chaste conjugal act which occasioned the Immaculate Conception of the Mother of God had not been, God's whole plan for our redemption would have been thwarted. This is quite an overwhelming thought for those who might desire to practice total continence — against God's will.

This is not an argument against total continence; if we are sure that continence is God's will for us. Rather it is but an assurance for those who might be tempted to abandon the road to perfection because of the mistaken notion that continence alone perfects chastity and so is a necessary requirement for union with God.

There is a saying among the married: "If God made anything better (than the physical expression of conjugal love) He kept it for Himself." In this saying there is more truth than jest;

for chaste conjugal love at its best is only an imperfect reflection of divine love, the infinite love of God for Himself.

If we who are married are caught up in this current of divine love, we are simultaneously caught up in the certitude that here is the something which God has kept, and which is infinitely better than the physical expression of conjugal love.

It is from this realization that the desire to practice continence springs. It is not so much the foregoing of the legitimate pleasure of sex in the spirit of mortification, but rather the desire to abandon one thing for that which is infinitely better. The soul who has quenched her thirst at the fountain of living waters no longer suffers from the thirst of sensuality.

And so it must be concluded that the active practice of the virtue of chastity is as important for the married as it is for those in any other state in life. Without chastity even the legitimate use of sex in marriage is in danger of degenerating into unbridled lust. On the other hand, conjugal love safeguarded by chastity may become the ladder upon which we shall climb to God and finally, arriving in heaven, bringing along with us all the souls who are the fruit of our chaste conjugal love.

11

REFLECTIONS ON HUMILITY

In Mary you will find a humility which manifests her loving submission to St. Joseph, her patient resignation to the dispositions — so often hard and painful — of Divine Providence, her affability and charity toward all those who came to the humble home of Nazareth (Pius XII, May 3, 1939).

HUMILITY

We have a rather painful complex about humility. As wives and mothers we know that we should be humble; as good Catholic wives and mothers, we wonder if we really are. Even the world pays sentimental tribute to our humility; our humble homes, the humble tasks we perform, the humble services we render in our humble vocation as housewives. With all the experience accredited to us we should be proficient in the practice of humility. We suspect though, that we are not. If we are truthful we are forced to admit that although a lot of our tasks are humiliating, instead of teaching us true humility, they merely injure our pride.

Yet we want to be humble, for we know that hidden in true humility is the secret of true sanctity. Our difficulty, though, lies in the fact that true humility keeps herself so well hidden that we find it almost impossible to gain entrance into her secret domain. So we cut for ourselves a pattern which seems

172

to fit our conception of humility; we strive to conform ourselves to this pattern, then find that what we thought was humility is nothing more than her counterfeit, false humility; pride turned inside out!

We need a plenitude of God's grace to understand humility; we need a superabundance of God's grace to practice humility. And so we falter, for we are not full of grace as was our heavenly Mother and perfect model of humility when she lived her hidden life in Nazareth. We falter in trying to practice the lessons in humility which she left for us to follow. We falter for even as we approach Mary's humility we are perplexed; it remains so elusive. Her charity, and purity, and resignation we seem to understand more clearly, but her humility seems always to elude us.

The trouble with most of us is that we try an intellectual approach to humility. We try to capture humility by reasoning and rationalization. If pride is diametrically opposed to humility, we reason, then we are humble if we constantly belittle ourselves. We may convince ourselves that self-belittlement is true humility, but we cannot be very happy in this conviction, and looking into Mary's life for the truth of this conviction we cannot find it. We just cannot imagine that our Lady ever belittled herself. She knew that she was the Mother of God and it is impossible for us to believe that she ever apologized for having accepted this sublime privilege. We know, rather, from her *Magnificat* that she gloried in her divine maternity. She knew also that her virginal motherhood set her apart from all of us, and that because of it all generations would call her blessed. Such a statement coming from the lips of our Lady was spoken in perfect humility; a similar remark coming from us might rightly be prompted by inordinate pride. And so we may turn away from Mary because of our inability to reconcile two such apparent contradictions.

If we are still interested and curious about humility, we may turn from our Lady to the dictionary. That is not much help, for the definition of humility ranges all the way from meekness and modesty to timidity and abject servility. So we find ourselves back again at the feet of Mary. Meekness and modesty we know she claims as her own, but try as we might we cannot consider timidity and abject servility as synonymous with humility — at least not with Mary's perfect humility. We know that the life which earned for her the title of Queen of Martyrs demanded a heroic courage; the service that she rendered to God was a total gift of herself, given generously and joyfully. There was nothing timid nor degrading about her humility. Must our humility differ from hers, because we are sinful and Mary was not? Must our humility always be tinged with pride?

Sooner or later we must discover that the path leading to true humility is blocked with the very reasoning, rationalizing, and knowledge upon which we had depended to show us the way. In encountering this blockade we may spend the rest of our lives trying to surmount it, to dig under it, or to work our way around it. And we may die in the attempt. Or we may see this obstacle, realize that we can never surmount it, make an inglorious retreat, and in retreating, find to our astonishment that the key for unlocking the secret of humility has been placed in our hands by the gracious hands of our Lady herself.

THE HANDMAID OF THE LORD

"Behold the handmaid of the Lord . . ." We may be saying the Angelus, we may have casually opened a book and these words are there before us. This phrase certainly is not new to us, we have had contact with it and have repeated it many times during the course of our Catholic life. But now, for a reason we cannot analyze, it has captured our attention in a way we cannot understand.

"Behold the handmaid of the Lord . . ." We find ourselves in spirit at the scene of the Annunciation. We have entered an unpretentious room and we see a girl, who seems hardly more than a child, kneeling in prayer. Already our faith has filled in her background and we know that here is God's darling; she who has been chosen from among all of us to be placed in a sinful world — alone — unspotted and sinless. We know that in her pure heart burns a more intense love for God than could be equaled by all the angels and saints. We know that her small hands, lifted in petition for the promised Redeemer, reached up into heaven and brought Him to us from the bosom of His Father. All of this we know about her, but as we gaze upon her we realize that she is aware of none of these things. She is kneeling in prayer rapt in the ecstasy of loving God with a love that brightens even the brightness of heaven, and offering herself over and over with the petition that this offering of herself might hasten the coming of the Messias.

Her prayer is answered. The Angel Gabriel stands before her. She wonders at his greeting and ponders it in her mind. But she does not question it. Instead she waits in respectful silence for the remainder of his message. One concern only she has — her precious virginity which she has already given to God by solemn vow.

So she says simply, "How shall this be done, because I know not man?"

The Archangel's answer is a mystery so sublime that the greatest theologians of the Church stand awed before the veil hiding it even from their scrutiny.

"The Holy Spirit shall come upon thee and the power of the Most High shall overshadow thee. And therefore also the Holy which shall be born of thee shall be called the Son of God" (Lk. 1:35).

A mystery beyond the realm of reason, yet this youthful Maid accepts it without the slightest hesitancy. She knows that, with God, all things are possible.

And we must wait breathless now, even as heaven does, for upon her answer depends God's whole plan of our redemption.

Mary's words are clear and without pretense: "Behold the

handmaid of the Lord; be it done to me according to thy word."

Our Redeemer is with us, hidden now in the tabernacle lovingly prepared for Him; resting sweetly in the warmth of His Mother's pure body. Mary's simple *fiat*, and the Word becomes flesh. The Incarnation is an actuality; the gate of heaven has been opened; in Mary the work of our salvation has begun.

We leave Mary's room now, but in reflecting upon the Annunciation we are lost in wonder and amazement. Our amazement centers upon the words of her consent: "Behold the handmaid of the Lord . . ." Our Lady seems to understand our bewilderment and gently prods us with the question *How would you have reacted in the same circumstance?*

We hardly need use our imagination! We would have wanted to know from the Archangel: Who are you? Where do you come from? Why did God send you to me? How could I ever discharge such an obligation? What is your opinion as to my worthiness? How can I be sure that what you say is true?

And we begin to understand now, why Mary can claim perfect humility as her own, and we cannot. For our lack of true humility evidenced in these numerous and pointless questions of ours would have confused even St. Gabriel, and the world probably would still be waiting for its Redeemer. We would have protested, we would have excused ourselves, we very likely would have refused. Mary did none of these things. She did none of them, not because of any opinion she had of herself, but because in her humility she relinquished her own opinion in favor of God's.

She knew that it was God's prerogative to choose His own Mother; Mary did not consider it her prerogative to question His choice. Furthermore, her faith assured her that God could not make a mistake; it assured her further that the loving acceptance of His will and her utter dependence upon Him would bring her to fulfill perfectly what she never could accomplish alone.

Mary consented to God's will simply and without question;

we spend our lives questioning God's will and rejecting it in favor of our own. We do not consider ourselves worthy of God's attention, nor of any of His special graces. Day after day He wills that the spiritual Incarnation of His Son take place in our soul; day after day we excuse ourselves from accepting this divine gift. We remain proud before God, yet Mary, despite ourselves, would teach even us to be humble.

OTHER FACETS OF THE GEM

Mary has given us our fundamental lesson in humility. We desire now to be humble and so we may begin again to reason and to rationalize. In doing so we must proceed prayerfully and cautiously, for any aggressive invasion of humility's secret domain may defeat its own purpose and fling us back against the stubborn wall of pride. For humility besides being one of the most elusive of all the virtues is also a subtle paradox of the spirit. In trying to discover humility we need take almost a negative approach by trying to pinpoint what it is not, rather than by trying to define exactly what it is.

From Mary we have learned that humility is not a belittling of ourselves, nor timidity, nor abject servility. We may go on to reason further that humility is not a disparaging of our talents; it is never filled with excuses; is never ostentatious; is never insulted, is never dissatisfied. What we need to learn now, is *why* humility is none of these things.

True humility is not a belittling of ourselves.

Although pride would not miss an opportunity to praise our excellence, there are days when we wake up with the bad taste of ourselves in our soul. On these days pride, in order to be appeased, would have us tell everyone how horrible we are. Not that pride really believes this, but because our associates' protestations to the contrary might reassure us again in the certainty pride had all the while: that we really are wonderful! Pride would convince us that we are generous and thoughtful and pious;

that we love God enough! But pride enjoys hearing others tell us so every now and then. It helps our morale and spurs us on to bigger and better accomplishments. However, pride does not like having its face uncovered and so it would convince us that we are being humble if we belittle everything we are or do. Pride's purpose is served if this kind of self-belittlement encourages praise and flattery from creatures, directed toward us.

True humility, on the contrary admits frankly that we are wonderful, then goes beyond this mere admission and rests upon the appreciation of why we are wonderful. She sees in our soul the reflection of God and so prostrates herself before the wonder of what we are. To humility we are tabernacles of the Most High, enclosed in the fragile temple of our mortal bodies, which demand respect and reverence as temples of the Holy Spirit. Never could humility belittle this handiwork of God, nor despise all the wonderful endowments with which this temple is adorned: the senses, the faculties, the God-given graces which allow us to partake of His divine life. But rather in her lowly estate, humility acknowledges all of these adornments, then returns them to God in thanksgiving with the petition that they be used only and always for His honor and glory and for our eternal salvation.

True humility is never a disparaging of our talents and abilities.

On the contrary we would be lacking in humility if we created a work of art, or gave a faultless concert, or produced a literary masterpiece, then tried to assure everyone that whatever we had done was no good simply because we had done it. If God has given us the talents and the abilities to do these things, He has also given us the discernment to evaluate their excellence. If whatever we have done is good and we describe the fruit of our labor with disparagement, we are lying and we know it. Even though we have missed the perfection for which we have aimed — since no artist can reach the perfection with which the divine Artist creates — yet find the reflection of His creative power in our endeavor, and deny it, we are falling again into pride. Pride would discount anything but our own ability and would look for assurance and approval from creatures. Pride would want to hear over and over the sugary language of praise and flattery while trying to deny the Creator who gave us these talents.

Humility allows our talents to be seen and to be appreciated. In showing them she cares neither that they be praised nor criticized. If what has been done is good, she knows it and admits it. The rest she gives to God, for she knows that our talents and abilities come from God and rest with Him. She prompts us to use them because in justice we must, or be held accountable for talents we have left unused. She strives to increase them that we may return to God over and above what have been given to us. Humility keeps our talents and abilities where they should be kept — hidden in God — and drawn upon as He sees fit.

True humility is never filled with excuses.

False humility and selfish pride would clothe our mistakes, our faults, and our failures with the most convincing excuses we can find. True humility would not, for she sees and recognizes these weaknesses when she encounters them and admits them truthfully and simply. She knows that as long as our soul is restrained within the flesh of our humanity that we are predisposed to error. However, she places the blame where it belongs — squarely with ourselves — for she knows that we enjoy being attuned to self much more often than we enjoy being attuned to God. But again humility uses even these mean transgressions profitably by referring them to the mercy of God, and using the experience gained from them as spiritual bridges to fling across the same pitfalls, should we encounter them in the future.

True humility is never timid.

Timidity would have us remain silent, even though we know we should be speaking for God and upholding His laws. Timidity would disguise itself as humility when it constrains us from taking a stand for what is right, necessary, or prudent. Timidity shies away from attention focused upon us and would remain unseen rather than run the risk of being criticized.

We may be timid by temperament, but even the timid grow strong in true humility. For although humility is retiring, she is never fearful of creatures nor of their criticisms, nor calumnies, nor misunderstandings. Humility rejoices rather in them, for these things strengthen her in the only fear she knows, the holy fear of God.

True humility is never ostentatious.

False humility would prompt us to be generous, especially with our money. It would insist that what we have given we have given to God; that our gift was given on condition that we remain unknown and without recognition and praise. And when recognition and praise are withheld we complain until everyone knows what we have given, the reason it was given, and our resentment at not being appreciated.

Prompted by true humility, we give generously of ourselves, our time, and our gifts. Humility gives everything she is able to give when she is aware of the need. Her gifts are given on no condition at all and with no strings attached. She gives simply because she loves God and what she gives, she gives to God, and always her gifts remain between her and God alone.

True humility is never insulted.

Humility is never insulted for the simple reason that true humility lacks the ability to be insulted. She respects everyone's opinion whether that opinion agrees with ours or not. Only pride can be insulted, for pride stays busy all our lives trying to paint a false picture of what we really are. If someone strips off the paint which pride has so carefully applied, we are insulted! Humility cannot be insulted for she gives the work of painting what we really are to God. She knows that whatever is beautiful in us is God's work and that He is completing in us a masterpiece which bears His image and likeness. If we deface this picture with clashing off-color daubings of our own, humility is grateful for the stinging application of truth which restores the image again to its original beauty.

True humility is never dissatisfied, and so she never complains.

Only pride seeks to assuage restless boredom and dissatisfaction by accumulating everything it can grasp in the way of material perfection, and prompts us to complain that nothing is good enough to please our discriminating taste. On the other hand, humility does not waste energy by forever picking and choosing, but accepts joyfully everything, or nothing, which providentially comes our way. Humility accepts all things as coming from the hand of God and receives them, not as our just due, but always with a sense of grateful wonder that God should continually show His paternal solicitude toward us. Humility would keep us happy with a crust of dry bread even if we saw everyone around us feasting. Humility would be grateful even for a crust, and that God had remembered to give it to us. She would not be envious of those who have more than we have, rejoicing rather, in others' plenty for she realizes and acknowledges that everyone else is more deserving of God's bounty than we are.

True humility is not abject servility.

Pride would tempt us to forego the active practice of humility by trying to convince us that humility is degrading. Pride would describe humility as having us cringing before God and men; as demanding only the meanest and distasteful services from us; of keeping us starved for lack of appreciation. Humility scorns this opinion pride has of her, for she knows that within her is contained the joy which uplifts and glorifies our services, no matter how distasteful and monotonous they may seem. Humility keeps all our tasks well ordered so that as we look over our day's schedule all of our work is muted and blended together into one loving sacrifice. All the things we like to do take no precedence over those tasks which pride would color with impatience and resentment. In working along with us, humility serves God first; then our family, friends, and neighbors in God — and our own selfish will, not at all.

Humility is silent.

But there is nothing humiliating about the silence of humility.

Silence is humiliating only when it lacks the perfection of true humility; when, for example, silence is imposed upon us by prudence or by obedience as it would be should we suffer from the rash judgment of others. To suffer such an injury (either real or imagined) is indeed humiliating and silence would seem almost to enslave the soul in rebellion and disquiet.

We react thus to imposed silence because we are still so imperfect in humility. Pride grows restive and would speak in order to glean consolation and sympathy from anyone who might listen. Pride would seek to highlight our own charity, even at the expense of another's. And yet, in the light of true humility, what right have we to judge the motives of others while we ourselves resent being judged?

And so again, we must turn to Mary for our lesson. We must learn from her how to suffer the humiliation of silence in order that we may learn also how to practice the perfect silence of humility.

Mary suffered from the most painful kind of misunderstanding that a sinless virgin could suffer — and from the one creature on earth whom she loved and respected most: her husband Joseph. What anguish must have been hers in sensing his tortuous doubts which could not reconcile her apparent virtue with her obvious pregnancy. In the light of human reasoning she stood accused. She could have explained, yet in the *darkness* of human reasoning, her explanation would have seemed a fabrication to cover guilt.

Mary remained silent. Without resentment, without the consolation of human understanding — and God made all things right for her.

And this Mary will teach us: that the perfect silence of humility is not the prohibition to speak, but humility's most eloquent expression. Unheard by creatures, it ascends to the very throne of God as the perfect song of love and sacrifice.

If we would imitate Mary and through this imitation come closer to God, we cannot strive merely for the perfection of the virtue of humility, hoping that the rest of the virtues will take care of themselves. We cannot even begin to practice humility much less rejoice in being humble, if we neglect any of the other virtues. Humility is integrally bound up with all the other virtues and its depth and perfection is proportionate with the practice and perfection of all the virtues, both theological and moral.

Pride is considered the root of all our sins. Humility is directly opposed to pride and thus humility can be likened to the fertile soil into which the virtues plunge their roots, are held, nourished and reach fruition. And just as pride is not always apparent in individual sins, yet is part of them, so also humility does not always manifest herself in the individual virtues. Humility remains hidden in much the same way that the rich earth is hidden from the admirer of a garden in full bloom. Yet the one enjoying the beauty of the summer garden knows that without the soil there would be no plants, no blossoms, no garden at all.

And so humility, hidden in her own retirement, prefers to remain in the lowest place, content to be unrecognized and unappreciated; intent only in being always the true handmaid of the Lord. Worshiping him, loving him, serving him and reminding us always that we are creatures and as such we are wholly dependent upon God, our Creator for our spiritual and temporal welfare. That in ourselves we are nothing, that by ourselves we can do nothing; but that in God all things can be accomplished in us.

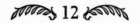

12

THE RING AND THE CROSS

"We are living in difficult times. Perhaps it will not always be possible to give children the comfortable, pleasant life that one dreams of for them or to make them peaceful or satisfied through the goods one would like to secure for them in addition to their daily bread. . . .

"But more than any earthly goods, which cannot even for the powerful and the feasters, ever transform this valley of tears into a heaven of delight, it is the parents who must give their children and heirs more valuable things, the BREAD AND WEALTH OF FAITH; the atmosphere of hope and charity; the incentive to a courageous and steadfast Christian life in which the sacred duties of fathers and mothers, conscious of the loftiness of the parenthood granted them by Heaven, will make them (the children) grow up and improve before God and their fellow creatures" (Address to Newlyweds — Pius XII, March, 1941).

For those of us who are married the ring is a symbol. It is the cross which is the reality. Whether the wedding ring is simple or ornate it is still only a symbol. No matter how little or how much material wealth it represents, it can never be used as a magic key to open the gates of a worldly paradise. It is only when we live out our marriage vocation in the light of the cross that our vocation becomes the source of our happiness on earth and our everlasting happiness in heaven.

What is worse than living a life without purpose unless it is living a vocation for the wrong purpose? God made us to know Him, to love Him and to serve Him in this life and to be happy with Him in eternity. This is the divine purpose of our life. It is also the divine purpose of our marriage — but with an even greater responsibility — for this divine purpose must be carried out and broadened to include the souls of those entrusted to our care: the souls of husband and children. To ignore or neglect this responsibility is to betray the trust God has given us as wives and mothers.

We know that we are living in difficult times. We are learning that the words of men which promise us peace and temporal security are anything but the truth. We are learning that the material advantages we struggle to give our children are failing to nourish and strengthen their characters because their souls are consequently suffering from spiritual malnutrition.

As Catholics we have been given the fundamental laws of God and of the Church along with the actual and sanctifying graces of the sacraments. All of these spiritual helps have been placed at our disposal to assure the spiritual success not only of our lives, but of our vocation as well. It is how we use these graces which makes the difference between the success or failure of our lives — of our vocation.

Unless our marriage is built upon the solid foundation of Christian principles; unless we strive for personal generosity in conforming our will to God's; unless we embrace the cross in the form of our own personal responsibilities; unless personal virtue is the shining raiment of our souls, our vocation as wives and mothers will fail in the eyes of God.

This aspect of our vocation is the cross in our life.

Voluntarily embracing this cross for Christ, and in union with Him, may seem repugnant to us, yet we need only to remember that embracing the cross for us was also repugnant to Christ. However, once the mystical cross of our vocation is embraced and carried generously and perseveringly we begin to realize the serene joyfulness of our marriage vocation. Living in such a way not only guarantees the spiritual success of the marriage vocation, we will know that it is a spiritual success.

God will reveal His pleasure in us by the resulting spiritual security and peace of soul which will be ours. We will see evidence of this success in the increased harmony in our homes; in the spiritual growth and maturity of the souls of those entrusted to our care, and all of which can come only from living in the light of the cross and in union with Christ.